SINGLE VOICES

SINGLE VOICES

Editors
Bruce Yoder and Imo Jeanne Yoder

Foreword by Jerry Jones

HERALD PRESS
Scottdale, Pennsylvania
Kitchener, Ontario
1982

Library of Congress Cataloging in Publication Data
Main entry under title:

Single voices.

   Bibliography: p.
   Contents: Single in a married society / Imo Jeanne Yoder—Singleness and relationships / Dorothy Gish—Singleness and professionalism / Melvin Lehman—[etc.]
   1. Single people—United States—Addresses, essays, lectures. 2. Single people—United States—Religious life—Addresses, essays, lectures. I. Yoder, Bruce, 1949-   . II. Yoder, Imo Jeanne, 1943-
HQ800.4.U6S55   305'.90652   82-3002
ISBN 0-8361-1998-3 (pbk.)   AACR2

SINGLE VOICES
Copyright © 1982 by Herald Press, Scottdale, Pa. 15683
   Published simultaneously in Canada by Herald Press, Kitchener, Ont. N2G 4M5
Library of Congress Catalog Card Number: 82-3002
International Standard Book Number: 0-8361-1998-3
Printed in the United States of America
Design: Alice Shetler

82 83 84 85 86 87 88 12 11 10 9 8 7 6 5 4 3 2 1

Contents

Foreword by Jerry Jones 7
Preface 9

1. Singleness and Relationships
   From Rebellion to Celebration 15
   Dorothy Gish
2. Singleness and Professionalism
   Rejection Slips and Spaghetti Suppers 27
   Melvin Lehman
3. Single in a Married Society
   Where Is My Family? 35
   Imo Jeanne Yoder
4. Singleness and Scripture
   Bible Stories for Singles 51
   Lois Janzen
5. Singleness and Sexuality
   A Gift from God 62
   Martha Smith Good
6. Singleness and the Church
   Models for Singles Ministries 73
   Herta Funk
7. Singleness and Spirituality
   Holy Loneliness 82
   Bruce Yoder

Reflection and Discussion Guide 97
Bibliography 121
The Writers 127

Foreword

According to an old Yiddish proverb, "It's not good to be alone, even in paradise." But apparently Yiddish is not spoken much (or at least understood) these days. *Time* magazine recently reported that the 1980 census showed 59 million unmarried adults in America. In addition, the U.S. Census Bureau projects that by 1985 over one half of all American adults will be single.

Staggering! And even more startling is the fact that before long even these statistics will be out-of-date. The numbers continue to climb. Our society is changing profoundly, especially as it relates to our traditional understanding of the word "family."

As I read through *Single Voices* for the first time, I was impressed by the way the reader is continually reminded that we are all "family" in the body of Christ. Dorothy Gish says it well in chapter one, "As Christians we have an obligation to live in belonging."

I was also impressed at the thoroughness with which a wide range of subject matter is covered. If you do as I did, you will underline many statements and will write many notes in the margins as you read this book. It is filled with excellent advice and helpful food for thought.

Even though each chapter is written by a separate individual, I sense a continuity throughout—a calling to each of us, whether we are married or single, really to be a part of each other's lives. The authors invite us to live in community as Jesus called us to live in the New Testament.

Each chapter and each writer brings a fresh voice to the subject of singleness. The authors are not bogged down in traditional, time-worn phrases or thought patterns. I gained a solid respect and appreciation for each of the writers. Each of them has personally wrestled (or is wrestling) through the issues of singleness. These writers are thinkers. They have enriched my understandings and the quality of my own life.

Regardless of your marital status, you will find *Single Voices* one of the best books available today on the "single life"—refreshing, stimulating, thought provoking, and genuinely helpful.

> *Jerry Jones*, Editor *Solo* Magazine
> Bartlesville, Oklahoma
> March 16, 1982

Preface

Single persons slip through the cracks of the institutional church with barely a whisper of distress being sounded by either the church or the individuals. At least that has been the case until recent years, though, sadly, it is still too often true. The particular pastoral and social needs and issues of single individuals tend to be passed over. The family-oriented ministries of the church are exhausted in caring for husbands, wives, and children, who have an increasingly difficult time coping with the forces of our culture that threaten the family unit and undercut its primary commitments. It is these singleness needs and issues that this book seeks to address within the context of the church, the family of God composed of persons who are single as well as those who are married.

Individuals may be single by decision, default, divorce, or death. Those who are single after having been married have certain needs and experiences through which to work that may not be shared by those who have never been married. Yet they do not stand utterly alone. The common ground of singleness is not a small plot. All who are single share much, whatever the cause of their singleness. It is that common ground, that shared experience, out of which this book grows.

All of the authors but one are single. Martha Smith Good, the one exception, was single all of her adult life until her recent marriage at which time she also became the mother of teenagers. All of the authors speak from within the Christian church. *Single Voices*, thus, is not only about the life of singleness within the church, it is also written by men and women who have lived that life. It is the authentic sharing of experience and reflection upon that experience that allows others to explore in their own lives the issues that are raised.

The life of singleness is viewed from seven different perspectives in the following chapters. No one view sees all that there is to see. Nor, for that matter, does the composite picture reveal all that there is within the world of singleness. It is but one frame of a movie, one stone in a mosaic. The life of any group within the Christian church is too complex to be handled with such a brief effort, especially as the life of that small group is seen in relationship to the larger group, the church. Rather than an exhaustive effort, we offer seven exploratory steps. The intent is to move toward correcting the imbalance of ministries within the church and closing the cracks through which no person in a caring community should fall.

Three of the chapters deal with singleness issues that are directly related to the church—Scripture, spirituality, and models of ministry. Three address concerns that would be more common to all singles, though the issues are spoken to within the context of the Christian church. These topics are sexuality, relationships, and professional life. The remaining chapter examines both church and societal forces that affect the development of a single person's identity.

Three themes emerge as these seven steps are taken. The first and most obvious is that single voices in the church are speaking out in a new way. Single persons want to be within the church as full members, active participants, completely accepted as brothers and sisters in the family who will shoulder responsibilities as well as share blessings. We have no desire to stand on the edge and watch, to be a spectator who applauds or criticizes. Single persons want to be in the heart of the church.

The second is that the common ground on which single persons stand is also shared by many who are married. Marital status has little or nothing to say about our needs for wholeness, for self-acceptance, or for close friendships. Marital status does not determine our acceptance of our sexuality or our spirituality. These items, as well as others, are not the concern of single persons because they are single but because they are human. The more deeply we move into ourselves, the more we see how much we are like one another. The shape of the problem may vary, the inflection of the question may differ, but the concerns that are raised in the depths of the life of the single person within the church are the same as those in the life of one who is married. Love, fidelity, loneliness, wholeness—these are human matters with which all Christians deal.

The third theme that takes shape is that singleness is an option for Christians. No rosy pictures are painted here, yet one can see that the choice to be single can be a thoroughly Christian commitment. In fact, several essays point in the direction to which some biblical material also directs us, namely that such a choice may be preferable to marriage. Or, to use the phrase of one Mennonite theologian, it may be that "marriage is fine but singleness is better."

Together, married Christians and single Christians form the church. By and large they share the common experiences of life. And where those experiences differ, quite often they each have in their hands one half of the whole. They need each other to be complete. The clearer, stronger voice of the single population within the church is not meant to overpower the other voice already present. It is meant only to be heard. As single and married Christians speak and listen to one another more steps can be taken together to strengthen the love and close the gaps, both of which are present within the church.

For groups who use this book we want to help that discussion take place by including a reflection and discussion section beginning on page 97.

We acknowledge with gratitude the many people who have supported the writing of this book. Singles particularly have inspired the creation of *Single Voices* by mentioning many concerns.

One person, who was single in the early stages of this book, deserves special recognition for contributing to the preliminary preparation for this book. Clair Hochstetler, Eastern VS administrator for Mennonite Board of Missions, remained involved with this project until Herald Press and the coeditors agreed to pick it up. His vision that we "facilitate interdependence and caring relationships among all persons in the church" inspired the creation of this book.

Bruce Yoder
Richmond, Virginia

Imo Jeanne Yoder
Harrisonburg, Virginia

SINGLE VOICES

Chapter 1

Singleness and Relationships

From Rebellion to Celebration

By Dorothy Gish

"Promise me that I'll be happy if I don't get married!" wailed the tall, willowy Southern belle college junior. Though socially active and getting acceptable grades, she was emotionally distraught because she'd so far failed to catch a husband. Like many people today, this young lady thought that her happiness and fulfillment depended on others. It is true that we do need others. The single as a self-sufficient, independent person who never admits to needing others is not the epitome of liberation. That kind of isolation is the epitome of sin which separates us from our Creator and our fellow creatures. God has provided for us the privilege of living in belonging with him. Closely related to that privilege is the obligation to live in belonging with his family.

Although we do need others, trying to find our happiness and fulfillment in another person destroys nourishing relationships because we make impossible demands on them. When people look only to others to fill them up, they feel unhappy, lonely, and incomplete. They have little except needs and desires to offer any relationship. Many singles try to make relations with others a substitute for meeting their own inner needs. Indeed, superficial relationships can be used as an escape from coming to terms with self. But an honest interest in being nourishing to others is not part of such relationships.

Circumstances and others do affect us. But it is alienation from self that causes unhappiness and loneliness. Thus the responsibility for unhappiness and loneliness rests primarily with the unhappy, lonely person. Only when one has come to terms with oneself is it possible to participate in the give-and-take of healthy relationships.

Achieving the mutuality necessary for nourishing and satisfying relationships doesn't happen automatically. In fact, it is a lifelong process. However, some identifiable developmental stages are involved in coming to terms with singleness. The process frequently begins with rebellion.

The stage of rebellion is exemplified by the woman whose attitude says, "I'm going to get married, no matter whom I have to settle for." Someone once assured me that "there's a lid crooked enough to fit every pot!" Also in the rebellion stage would be the man who acts like a Don Juan, snug in the confidence that he is God's gift to women.

Viewing their marital status as a basic cause of their problems, they rebel against being single. This rebellion is primarily an angry striking out at self but often others get hit in the process. Thus interpersonal relationships are affected. One result is that frequently persons of the opposite sex are reduced to sex objects because they are consciously or unconsciously assessed as possible mate material. Getting their attention or approval becomes extremely important. Dating, with its best-foot-forward stance, assumes all the ritual and posturings of a mating dance. It is almost impossible to learn to know the real person behind all the masks and trappings.

From Rebellion to Celebration / 17

Nor is it unusual for persons going from this stage directly into marriage to wake up after the honeymoon to find that their spouse is a virtual stranger.

Just as people of the opposite sex are reduced to spouse possibilities, one's own sex is analyzed largely in terms of how they relate to the other sex. Two basic categories emerge: competitors and accomplices.

June schemed many ways to keep from having her dates pick her up at home because they found her youngish mother too attractive. Jim refused all requests for double dates because he had learned from sad experience that you "really couldn't trust other men." While neither Jane nor Jim realized it, their discomfort with others arose largely out of seeing others as in competition with them for a spouse.

But not everyone is a competitor. Those who have connections with eligible friends or relatives can become accomplices. There are some who are extremely "helpful." Soon after their mother died, eight-year-old Sally and 10-year-old Susie found a number of young ladies who suddenly were remarkably friendly. Frequently others play the role of accomplice even when the one "helped" doesn't desire assistance. Pleasant, good-looking, thirtyish, and single, Fred confessed that he dreaded Sunday nights at his church. Various concerned members would invite young women to the service. The interaction after the service took on something of an "auction-block" atmosphere as the eligible women were presented to him.

A person who is desperate to find a mate cannot develop good relationships with others. Incomplete, unhappy, and lonely, these singles search for a "better half" to fulfill them. Unfortunately, these worse halves on the loose have little to offer except their own needs and desires. Thus, their search is doomed to failure. The best seems to be a tragic possibility of finding an equally needy, unhappy, and unfulfilled person.

The stage beyond rebellion is depression. At this stage, one feels like a reject. It is the "Something's wrong with me, I just don't have what it takes" feeling, because as one writer put it, "Nobody chose me; I didn't quite make it. Somebody else was just a little something more." For some Christians this depression stage may also be connected with a "mad at God" stage. Recently a tearful woman passionately confessed, "I am a committed Christian. I have devotions every day, and I am vitally involved in the church. But right now I'm mad at God. I gave him all I have and he turns around and withholds from me someone to love and care for. He sees that I really need a husband, why doesn't he let me have one?"

In our society, depression is well fed by the myth of fulfillment and the myth of normality. Communicated extensively by the mass media of our day, the myth of fulfillment proclaims that one cannot find happiness and fulfillment unless one finds the right person to love. Whereas the mass media are the largest purveyors of the fulfillment myth, individuals most extensively communicate the myth of normality. Verbally and nonverbally they clearly convey society's message: "All normal, well-adjusted people get married."

At the depression stage, one implicitly views the opposite sex as superior beings who have the power to choose or to refuse. The fact that one is not chosen seems to imply that one is not good enough. Or if one who proposes is refused, the implication is that the proposer isn't "good enough."

One's own sex is again divided into two groups: those who made it and those who didn't. There is frequently an attempt to discredit the success of those who made it (the married): "Guess how she got such a nice guy!" or "Well, he finally managed to find someone who'd have him but she's not exactly what you'd call a 'find'!" The unmarried (those who didn't make it) provide small comfort. Clearly not a case of "misery loves company," these "losers" frequently impel other "losers" to oneupmanship: "I sure have a better figure than she does, and I've got a brain, too"; "I'm in a higher-income bracket than he is, and I'm not that bad looking either."

The stage after depression, a passive response to not making it, takes one to the more active behavior of rejection. It says, in effect, that since I didn't make it from "single file to center aisle" I'm going to reject all aisles—left, right, and center. This rejection sometimes takes the form of a denial of the desire for marriage. That denial may be expressed in many ways: from an overt, brassy "Marriage? Who needs it!" to a more subtle bragging, "What could a man add to my life that I don't already have?" I must admit that there are times when, faced with the perpetual question about my lack of a spouse, I am tempted to sarcasm: "Since there obviously aren't enough men to go around, I thought I'd be noble and leave them for those like you, who really need them."

A person at the stage of rejection views the opposite sex as a sort of separate and rather treacherous species because they are quite adept at using others. Since getting involved often results in being used or hurt, it is best to keep one's distance. While more trustworthy, one's own sex is frequently bogged down with marital concerns and so are not much help.

At the next stage, repression, the rejection of marriage is no longer overt and obvious. Now marriage is just something one simply does not think about. The repressed desires, however, come out in many ways. For some it takes the form of sublimation to a job or a career. As I look back now, I recognize that part of my motivation for getting a doctorate ran something like: "Anyone can get a husband, but not everyone can get a PhD." Sometimes repression is expressed through constantly driving to be on top, getting one degree after another or striving for continuous achievement or constant recognition. For some singles, repression takes the form of playing martyr to parents or other obligations. Someone has well said that the role of martyr might be enjoyable for the person playing it, but it is boring to everyone else.

With marital concerns suppressed, one is able to view others somewhat asexually and thus is free to relate to either sex. Since one is concerned with keeping life so full that feelings don't have time to intrude, others become friends helping to fill the schedule and perhaps to get ahead professionally. Because they are so busy and their life is so full, some singles at this stage may be seen by others (or even see themselves) as being satisfied with singleness.

But real satisfaction can only come with the next step: acceptance. I believe that it is quite likely not possible to attain this stage without some degree of self-acceptance. In this area the Christian has a tremendous advantage. God created us as we are. He loves us and accepts us as we are. Realizing this frees us from the drive to try to make ourselves acceptable.

In regard to acceptance of the single state, there is frequently a crisis time when acceptance comes. It does not come easily and some struggle harder than others. But acceptance comes only at the point where we can honestly say to the Lord: "Okay, I really prefer to be married. That is what society expects and that's what people who have made it seem to have. I'd like to be in that group, but if it is your will for me not to be married, I accept that. I realize that you give different gifts to different people. To some you give the gift of marriage, to others the gift of singleness. Singleness is not a gift that I would have chosen, but if you have chosen it for me, then it must be good."

The stage of acceptance seems to be more easily achieved by those who have had the chance to say "No" or have received a negative reply to an invitation to marry. The woman who feels like she must wait to be chosen has an additional sense of helplessness and hopelessness. Still, she should remember that while she may not be able to choose to marry, she does have the freedom to choose not to marry. Each person has likely had some opportunity which could have led to marriage. Nearly anyone can find a spouse, if just anyone will do. So for whatever reason, a clear leading of the Lord, an I-hate-the-opposite-sex syndrome, or unrealistic idealism, one is single by choice. At the end of a singles' retreat, one person put it this way: "I'll take back with me . . . greater satisfaction with being single, seeing that I have chosen singleness as an option." Acceptance comes when one decides as Elva McAllaster's delightful book suggests that for whatever reason or duration one is *Free to Be Single*.[1]

The more one can accept oneself, the more one is able to accept others. Relating to others as real human beings with varying strengths and weaknesses, skills and ineptitudes, joys and sorrows, makes real friendships possible. To achieve this stage of acceptance is as far as many people ever get. I believe that one is not ready for marriage until one has personally reached this stage. However, for those to whom God gives the gift of marriage, acceptance is perhaps as far as they need to go for themselves. But, for singles, there are two further stages.

Affirmation is the step beyond acceptance. It says not only that I am single by choice, but that I am comfortable about that choice. Singleness is not just a downhill slide that I cannot prevent. Rather, it is a deliberate walk with the Lord. Indeed, it often becomes an uphill climb, but as long as the Lord and I are in it together, that's all that matters. An acquaintance put it this way: "I am satisfied with singleness because I look at it as God's *BEST* for me [now]." Her friend wrote: "God has a plan for my life, and now as a single person I am more free to be used of him in areas that I could not be if I were married."

At the stage of affirmation, one begins to realize some of the privileges and opportunities singleness affords. The control singles have of their time and money allows many freedoms denied a married person. A single is free from having to fill certain roles or live up to another's expectations in those roles. The opportunity for taking a low-paying job, or of giving long hours of service to others, is possible. Then, too, the single person has the freedom to give sacrificially without sacrificing the economic well-being of another. For example, a friend of mine gave to missions the money she could have used for the down payment on a house. Consequently, she still rents but no one else's well-being is jeopardized by that lack of equity. Additionally, there is the freedom for travel, long hours of study, privacy for meditation and reflection, and other personally enriching activities. Restrictions on where one goes, with whom, for what reasons and at what expense are not imposed by others but are chosen solely by the single person.

A friend is one of God's greatest gifts. Since God created us for communion and friendship, we are complete only in loving friendships with others. However, expecting everything from a friendship will lead to disappointment, for no human friend can fill the ultimate void in the human heart. Only God can do that.

But human friendship does open us by bringing us out of ourselves and freeing us from self-preoccupation. Thus it makes us more sensitive and responsive to others and to the Lord. In marriage one's habits and protective devices are challenged in the intensity of daily living with another person. The single needs some relationships affording a deep level of mutual sharing and self-exposure.

> The more I become at home with another in friendship, then, the more I get to know myself. In my vital relationships with others, I see myself in operation, and become aware of my faults, my sinfulness, as well as my good qualities. It is only in living a relationship that I learn my sinful tendencies to abuse a relationship. Until these sinful tendencies are unveiled and uprooted, my relationship with God will be hampered by them. By letting myself experience friendships deeply, I have my hidden sins revealed to me, which I would never have known otherwise. In the give-and-take of human relationships, in the friction of repeated encounters which make the sparks fly, I become aware of my rough edges and know what I must polish away. The person who is never involved with others, but withdraws into a shell, never learns either his strengths or his weaknesses.[2]

We all need friends with whom we can share experiences, thoughts, feelings, and confidences. Having friends we respond to and who respond to us, with whom we can share our joys and sorrows, makes the difference between enjoying being single and feeling miserable.

A single at the stage of affirmation is able to relate warmly and caringly to people of both sexes. In fact, it is essential for emotional well-being to have close friends of both sexes. As Christians we have an obligation to live in belonging. The celibate lifestyle does not free an individual from the duty of partnership and creative encounter with the opposite sex. For this to be possible, the single must have a healthy acceptance of his or her own sexuality.

It is true that there are risks in communication with another, but accepting one's body and one's sexuality as a normal part of one's humanity lessens the risk of abusing the emotional elements which are part of a relationship. It is possible to enjoy the friendship of the opposite sex without fear when we realize that friendship (or even sexual attraction) does not necessarily imply the need for genital interaction.

In friendships with the opposite sex, honesty and openness in the relationship can help offset the danger of one person reading more into the friendship than the other intended. Having more than one friend of the opposite sex might help to avoid the speculations of well-meaning friends or the suspicions and perhaps outright rumors about "being more than just friends!"

Friendship should bring gladness to both and make each more able to reach out to others. A truly loving relationship brings liberty and expansiveness. Ugly and imprisoning, possessiveness leads to confinement which kills friendship. By developing one's whole personality, a single can become a whole person capable of giving and taking freely in a healthy relationship with another. Every pain in a relationship should be a reminder of the lordship of Christ. Neither friends, nor possessions, nor accomplishments, nor anything else can provide security and fulfillment. Christ alone can do that. Loving reverence for others then results from appreciation of their true value as persons created by God.

The last and highest stage of singleness is that of celebration. This means not only being comfortable about one's choice, but actually thankful for it, able to say, "I am glad the Lord has allowed me to be single these years. In the future many things may change, even my marital status, but for now, I'm glad I'm single. I'm not going to squander that privilege by wasting my time moping around for a spouse to justify my existence, nor will I waste precious time dreaming about what might have been or may yet be. Rather, I'll celebrate by living each moment to the full, now."

One of the blessings of consecrated singleness is freedom from the excessive presence of loved ones. When one is continuously involved in meaningful relationships, being alone can have the nourishing quality of solitude. The resulting privacy can be refreshing and lead to a life enriched by solitary refinement. Solitude is being fully at home with oneself.

While solitude can enable one to learn to know the Lord and oneself better, for full maturity one also needs intimacy. Just as marriage does not equal full personhood, so intimacy does not equal sexual intercourse. Intimacy involves being fully one's self with someone else, being at home with someone else. Intimacy means being fully known and lovingly appreciated. Thus there is no fear of rejection nor need to do things to win the other's approval. Because intimacy is a love which accepts one fully even when it sees imperfections, it patiently nurtures whatever is imperfect and appreciatively draws out the potentialities for good.

Yet, even in that intimacy one must always recognize the right of others to have an equally close relationship with that friend. Marriage alone has the unique relationship of belonging.

> In marriage there is a fusion of two personalities expressed in the one-flesh union. In friendship the two personalities run

side by side, the more enriched for knowing each other, mutually strengthened by their closeness but nevertheless separate....[3]

While not easy, it is possible for singles to be satisfied—even to the point of celebrating their choice of singleness. For Christians, the most important person in their lives was single for all 33 years of his earthly life. Whatever one's marital status, life with him can indeed be a celebration.

The stages of developing the kind of relationships which enable one to be satisfyingly single begin with rejection and end with celebration. It is likely that no one always lives at the stage of celebration. But once having achieved it, one knows the way to return to it. One might experience these stages in cycles. Perhaps the stages are not even mutually exclusive. But it is possible to work through a personal acceptance of singleness from a rebellious "No way!" through the "Yuk!" of depression, past the "Count me out!" rejection, beyond a repressive "Duh!" to the "Okay" acceptance and even to the affirmative "Right on!" with an occasional celebrative "Whoopee!"

Notes

1. Elva McAllaster, *Free to Be Single* (Chappaqua, N.Y.: Christian Herald, 1979).

2. Paul Hinnebusch, *Friendship in the Lord* (Notre Dame: Ave Maria Press, 1974), p. 66.

3. Margaret Evening, *Who Walk Alone* (Downers Grove, Ill.: InterVarsity Press, 1947), p. 47.

Chapter 2

Singleness and Professionalism

Rejection Slips and Spaghetti Suppers
By Melvin Lehman

I'm not sure precisely when it happened, but sometime within the past year or so I found myself actually looking forward to Monday mornings when I go back to work. My job involves writing and editing materials about refugees. Some of the parts of my job which I find very interesting are: talking to refugees, reading several newspapers from the United States and numerous other publications from around the world for news about refugees, choosing photographs, writing newsletters under deadlines, editing publications about refugees and human rights issues, and going to meetings. I even find reading memos interesting. I often work overtime and Saturdays. I find my work very exciting and rewarding.

I also happen to be a single person.

What is the relationship between those two aspects of my life: my profession and the fact that I am single?

That question got me thinking. Having a profession—in my case, writing—and being single are both significant parts of any person's life. What is the relationship between the two? Does one cause or lead to the other? Do those two aspects of my life create conflict? Are they complementary? Or all of the above?

At the outset, a few qualifications and definitions are in order.

For one thing, this essay will tend to be rather subjective and personal in nature. There is no well-established body of research and literature (at least that I am aware of) from which to draw reliable generalizations. Except to say that there are more singles around these days, few generalizations can be imposed on the many varied experiences of single people. Being free to be an individualist is one of the primary benefits of being single, and I would not want to subtract from that advantage by promoting generalities. Instead, I will be making somewhat personalized observations with the hope that others can identify with at least some of them.

By way of terminology, "single" is relatively easy to define. It is, obviously, the state of not being married.

"Profession" is a bit harder to define. I tend to be liberally inclusive in defining this term. The old habit of equating "profession" with such jobs as doctor and lawyer is far too limited. I believe any job in which one has to make informed decisions is a profession. That simple definition includes quite a few of us.

Is there a causal relationship between having a profession and being single? It could be argued that some professions are so demanding that they lead to putting off marriage or actually contribute to divorce in some cases. I believe these are isolated instances, however. A person's decision to have a career probably has minimal effect on the decision to get married. What is more probable is that a person who remains single is more likely to pursue a professional career.

The fact that a person is single may influence the way one

approaches one's profession, and it may also influence the kind of profession one chooses. Being single has the advantage of requiring less immediate family responsibility and allowing for more risk-taking in one's career. If one's career is not immediately successful, one is not faced with the considerable demands of supporting a family.

The increasingly common practice in today's society of both parents working may be improving the possibility of risk-taking for one or both parents. Singles, however, have known this advantage for some time. If their profession is not working out well or they decide to change professions, they have more freedom to do so than married persons with families.

As a former academic and aspiring writer, I have experienced considerable freedom in developing my profession as a single person. There is, after all, no professional accreditation for writers and certainly no tenure. One becomes a writer over a period of years by writing. And there are plenty of rejection slips and budget spaghetti suppers along the way.

A theological point could be made here regarding singles within the larger church fellowship. If the theory is true that being single means having more freedom in regard to profession, it would follow that singles can bring that spirit of freedom to the church. The Christian life, after all, is partly one of discipline but more importantly one of freedom. So many times our churches are primarily family-oriented and they become absorbed in the process of well-ordered domestic life devoted to raising pious and devout children. The freedom we singles have should provide yeast for the larger church. Our having more options open and time to explore various ideas can make a real contribution to what is sometimes a rather methodical church life.

So far this essay has examined what possible effect our singleness can have on our professions. We now need to look at what effect our professions have on us as single people.

One of the most important aspects of being a single professional is a very simple but profound one: we come home alone at the end of the day. While at times that can be quite routine, at other times it can be most difficult. A profession, according to my earlier definition, is any job in which one needs to make informed decisions. Often those decisions are simple. At other times, they are difficult and ambiguous. And occasionally, we make the wrong decisions. It is at those times that coming home to an empty apartment is the hardest.

I do not have as naive a view of married life as to assume that one's spouse can utter magic words and make one's problems of the day evaporate. But I do believe that in a healthy marriage one can process one's ups and downs and put them in a broader context.

Singles, unfortunately, do not have the advantage of having that process to rely upon. At the end of a long, hard day we come home, alone, turn on the water for the spaghetti, and review the trouble of the day to ourselves. While we're making the spaghetti, we think to ourselves, if only I'd have done it differently. As we heat up the sauce we think, why hadn't I thought of that ahead of time? And then, while we're eating our meal alone (while watching "Family Feud"?) we think, next time, I'll know better, and I won't make *that* mistake again.

For evenings like this singles need friends. Friends are the greatest persons in the world to help one get through the rough spots. Next time, if you can, turn off the TV, call up a friend, spend a few bucks, and get together for supper. It is very important that singles have friends to process the ups and downs of life. If we don't have a family, friends are doubly important.

Another danger single professionals should be wary of is the insidious temptation to substitute professional accomplishments for genuine personal caring. We face the real temptation of becoming overachievers to substitute for personal affection. The danger is that we begin substituting professional accomplishments for all-natural, nutritious, homemade personal affection and love.

It is often easier to sit at one's desk and plow one's way through a difficult anonymous professional task than to cultivate intimate personal relationships with their built-in risk of disappointment and hurt along with the joy. Professional success and acknowledgement is infinitely more predictable. One does one's task with energy and intelligence and one is rewarded. It's usually just that simple.

Intimate personal relationships involving genuine love and caring are much more complicated. They take time and energy. And risk. Making it through graduate school guarantees one a diploma suitable for framing. Personal relationships carry no such guarantee. One may even be disappointed or hurt.

As busy, pragmatic singles, our temptation is to direct our energies to our professions where the rewards are predictable, and to avoid personal relationships where there is no similar guarantee.

Single professionals should be wary of another similar danger: substituting the camaraderie of professional friendships for the more intimate caring relationships we really need. This is not to suggest that professional friendships are of no consequence. On the contrary, they can be very meaningful. But often they can be mistaken for the deeper caring relationships we need.

One more danger needs to be duly noted. That is the danger of becoming enamored with the money we make. Some of us eating spaghetti suppers and paying off graduate school loans may be in somewhat less danger in this regard than others, but the danger exists nevertheless. We have, after all, a household of only one to support. What does one do if one has cash left over? Most of the blandishments of the "me generation" syndrome are too vulgar to be taken very seriously, but still the temptation of overindulgence exists. Further complicating the situation is the fact that some indulgence is appropriate. It is good and healthy to spend a little bit of money on a few material possessions. The problem comes in determining the line between moderation and excess, between occasional indulgence and overindulgence, between a healthy enjoyment of life's goodness and a crude conspicuous consumption.

One additional danger needs to be noted in regard to being single and being a professional: the temptation to neglect ourselves. That caution may seem a bit unusual immediately following a caution against overindulgence. Don't we, after all, have plenty of time on our hands to do interesting and enriching things like reading the classics and going to museums? Who, us, neglect ourselves? Aren't we prime candidates, on the contrary, for narcissism?

Perhaps. But more often, I believe, we don't love ourselves enough. We are usually so busy, so active, on so many committees, that we often don't have time to appreciate ourselves, to love ourselves, as we are in fact commanded to do. Sometimes, in our aloneness, we don't have persons to love us and to help us love ourselves. In our busyness we erect invisible walls against intimacy. When we fail to experience the love of others, we often have trouble loving ourselves.

We often don't take the time to just be happy and contented with who we are. The happiness we knew as children too often seems to disappear amid the responsibilities and tensions of our professions. We need to "become as children" and recapture the appropriate love of ourselves.

In order to do this, I believe friends are most important. All of us have many sides to our personalities and many needs. Our busy professions with their responsibilities can develop many important parts of our personalities, but not all of its parts. We need friends to develop that part of our personality which needs love and caring, affection and tenderness. Friends give us a community, a context. They give us the freedom to relax and be ourselves. Professions demand responsible decisions from us. Friends make demands, too, but of a different sort. They demand that we share, and trust, and give.

In an essay of this sort which tries to examine the relationship of being single and having a profession one must guard against placing too much importance on both singleness and a profession. Our singleness and our professions are only a part of our humanity, and those parts of our lives must be seen as part of our total self-understanding.

Several other categories of existence are equally important or more important to me than these two categories. I am a human being, a Christian, a nonconformist pacifist Mennonite, in addition to being a single writer. Each of us are sentient human beings with our needs to love and be loved, our successes and failures, our histories and futures, our developing spirituality, our at times boisterous egos, our shortcomings and our strengths.

As a writer, I may look up words in the dictionary more often than most people do, and worry about my deficiencies and lapses in sentence construction and grammar more often than most people do, but in the most important parts of life I am really not all that different from (or is it "than"?) other people. My singleness is an important part of my self-definition, but it is only a part.

As single persons, we are called to discover the fullness and richness of our humanity, to live out our calling with an almost reckless abandon. The fact that we are slightly outside the norm of the "tribe" as single adults should not become a stumbling block but rather it should give a special intensity to our search for our unique humanity. Our special perspective on life should be celebrated and affirmed.

Our professions should be a way of achieving that fullness of personhood. I can conceive of few things more dispiriting for a single person than to have a job one does not like, a job where one simply trades one's time for a weekly paycheck. The challenge and excitement of our calling in life should be a large part of our excitement about life in general.

Our Lord himself, it should be noted, was a single professional. He was a teacher, and he never married. He loved and was loved. He worked and studied hard, but he also, to the dismay of the religious establishment of his day, loved parties and celebrations. He had friends, both male and female. He was intoxicated with the goodness and richness of life.

Our challenge as singles is to find a similar love in life: of our work and of our neighbors and of our selves. And of God, the giver of all good things.

Chapter 3

Single in a Married Society

Where Is My Family?

By Imo Jeanne Yoder

"You lose. You drew the Old Maid card," jeered my best friend's older sister. It was bad enough to draw the card with the crochety old woman with spectacles, but to have this misfortune announced loudly enough so that the adults in the next room stopped their conversation was, at best, humilitating. I began to slink further and further into the big overstuffed chair which I was occupying. Suddenly, I decided that the best way to handle my feelings was to make a hasty exit. Pigtails bouncing, I shouted, "Someone has to draw the Old Maid card. Next time it might be you. So there."

Like many other children, I was taught that drawing this card in "real life" not only meant losing, but an extra bonus was having all of society's players treat you like a loser. Who sent me these messages? Many persons promoted such beliefs in my church and school. The most important source was community gossip, a form of social control designed to keep persons from deviating from formal and informal norms or rules. Persons in my church played the role of an extended family and helped me learn the rules very quickly.

One of the first rules I learned was that marriage was a must if one wanted to avoid being the object of community gossip.

I never questioned the emphasis on marriage and procreation, because it seemed to be a safeguard against the extinction of small, rural communities. Sociologist Vernon Jantzi sees a direct tie between marriage and economies based heavily on agriculture:

> In this kind of context, it became extremely important to marry, to produce the labor necessary to keep the economic enterprise afloat. Not only was the economic pressure to marry and have children, it also provided a way for a family to work its way out of poverty. Thus, having lots of children meant that one might be able to make the farm more productive and, therefore, generate greater income.[1]

In order to discover other factors that contributed to the pressure to marry and have children, we must trace religious influences in the larger society and sex-role socialization, as well as economic developments. After tracing these factors in historical sequence, the Christian views on marriage and procreation will be explored.

Several religious influences in the larger society have been important. The early medieval church viewed marriage as a concession to carnality made only to propagate the race. Therefore, celibacy was encouraged for priests and nuns. Menno Simons, the leader of the 16th-century Dutch Anabaptists, wrote that a priest "must be so pure and chaste in his conduct that he is not allowed to marry a wife, although the holy Scriptures allow it."[2]

This comment appears to be an attempt to justify the marriage of clergy rather than a comment discouraging singleness. His other writings emphasize the oneness of the body of Christ.[3] Scholars should research the treatment of singles by the 16th-century Anabaptists.

When the Puritans came to America they regarded marriage as a protection against immorality. From history books on Colonial America we learn that many New England towns put bachelors on two tax rolls. This was a result of the theory that "sin and iniquity ... ordinarily are the companions and consequences of the solitary life." Also, a bachelor could be required to live with families who were licensed to be responsible for his morals.[4] Frost, in his book, *The Quaker Family in Colonial America*, writes: "New Englanders saw the family as the foundation of church and state and insisted that single people, whom they viewed with some distrust, live in a family and submit to the authority of the father."[5]

But do economic factors still affect our norms regarding marriage in today's society? Yes, says Jantzi, but for different reasons:

> ... As our society has industrialized, particularly in the latter quarter of the century, the emphasis has become much more on capital, even in agriculture. Thus, the pressure to marry is still there from an economic source, but now with a different incentive. It becomes important at this point to accumulate capital rather than labor, thus one would hope to have a marriage that would combine two sources of capital and thereby generate the resources necessary for the new family unit to enjoy a high standard of living.[6]

Nuclear families (husband, wife, and children) replaced the extended family (grandparents, brothers, sisters, or other blood relatives) in society much earlier, but the industrial revolution altered its structure. The pattern which emerged was one of specialization within the family. The majority of husbands had the sole responsibility of breadwinning, while women became the caretakers of the children. Girls were encouraged to form a tentative identity, so they could form their identities around their husband and children. Little boys, on the other hand, were prepared for the breadwinning role.

This adaptation of the nuclear family not only divided the household, it left out singles, including single parents. According to some observers the nuclear family is a primary reason why we are not free to be single in today's society. Marriage has been the rite of passage into adulthood.

Experts disagree as to how we are taught our adult roles, but they do agree that children are socialized into their roles from an early age. Socialization is the process by which the infants, children, and adults learn the ways of a given society and culture and become functioning members of society.

Two important questions should be considered. What were the possibilities for role models in our social structure? What in our culture might have made us choose one model over another? Examples from my childhood may enable the reader to recall his or her own experiences. This discussion will deal with how we were socialized as children rather than how children are being socialized today.

If it were possible to recall the first two years of life, no doubt most of us would discover that we began to imitate everything our parents did by age two. By age three, children begin imitating the adult models around them, and, at times, they find others chuckling if they differ too much from the traditional sex roles.

> My favorite childhood activity was running a business, and over and over again, I kept getting the message from adults other than my parents that women do not run businesses. I

promptly informed these adults that I had in fact taught brother, who was playing the role of my husband, how to kiss the babies and take care of them. They always chuckled and said, "I wonder if he (my brother) will be masculine when he grows up."

Researchers of sex role development have concluded that girls, by the age of three, imitate their mothers, while little boys imitate the father role. In my own situation I could often be seen preaching in my play, since I had learned that my father's position had more power and status than my mother's. However, this example from my childhood at age four illustrates that one must conform to cultural norms in order to gain approval from peers:

> Pinning an old lace curtain on my head, I prepared to run down the aisle. My cousin informed me that now that I was a wife, I must become a mommy. I staged a protest and was on the verge of tears, but eventually gave in. Even though I did not want to have a baby right away because of my business interests, I succumbed to social pressure and gave birth to the traditional role of mother.

Storybooks reinforced the idea that women should remain in the home while men worked. Some of the books even showed the animals in rigid sex-defined roles. For example, I recall a book with father possum resting after a hard day's work, while mother possum fed the babies. Fairy tales perpetuated the myth that one must marry and ride off into the sunset in order to live happily ever after. Although my parents told me that romantic love is not a good basis for marriage, I learned somewhere along the way that bells would ring when I kissed the man of my dreams.

With the advent of mass media, particularly TV, stereotypic roles were reinforced. Even though double messages were received about the housewife role, because of the "dumb housewife" image, marriage had more appeal than being labeled an "old maid."

The other question which I still want to address is how socialization might make children choose one role model over another.

> As a child the role models I most admired were single women, who were missionaries. I soon began to hear derogatory comments about how this type of service was okay if you couldn't catch a man. Since these messages came from the adults in my church, I began to internalize these messages. When I was a teenager, I worked with the deaconesses, a kind of religious order for single women sponsored by the General Conference Mennonite Church. I was very impressed with these women as role models. However, every time I began talking about how much I admired these deaconesses, my mother began to talk about the joys of motherhood.

In spite of this socialization, which prepares us for marriage, the trend is changing in society. According to 1979 Census Bureau figures, there are approximately 55 million singles over the age of eighteen in the U.S. today. Sherry Andrews, in an article, "Why Is the Church Becoming Single-Minded," says, "By the end of this century—if current patterns continue—single adults will be the majority in the United States."[7] Although the number of persons who were living alone under the age of thirty-five increased from 1.5 to 4.3 million between 1970 and 1978, many researchers are cautious in saying this rate of increase will continue.

Developmentally, the years from twenty to twenty-eight are regarded as a time when the focus of one's life shifts from the "family of origin" to a new home base.[8] Therefore, it is the time period when one forms one's adult identity and establishes a lifestyle upon which initial choices are reevaluated. This time of reevaluation has been reported by many Christian singles, like other singles, to involve struggle with societal pressure, with family, and with oneself.

It would be difficult to determine how many singles under thirty-six are delaying marriage and how many are choosing singleness as an option. But researchers are suggesting two conclusions. The women's liberation movement has made singleness a much more attractive option for females, due to the oppression married women feel. Second, more professional jobs are open to women, hence more singles are entering professions. Jantzi says:

> At this point, the role of marriage does not have the same economic impact as it did in the earlier ... stages of our society. Thus, it seems to me that this is one of the things that would also predict that we will rethink our view of marriage in our society over the next number of decades. In fact, to enter a profession in our society at this point militates against marriage. The need to be able to freely move from one area of the country to another, to continually retool in one's profession, and to travel is antithetical to the kind of structure we have had in the past in marriage.[9]

Other writers in the field agree that we will have to rethink our view of marriage in the next decades. Peter J. Stein, one of the leading writers on singleness, says:

> Active experimentation with alternatives to the nuclear family underscores the discontent with marriage as a norm.... Evidence exists that singlehood is emerging as a social movement overlapping with other liberation movements, but in the process of developing a distinctive body of ideas.[10]

One of the first conditions for the emergence of a social

movement is a growing discontent with existing patterns. Second, the oppressed must be resocialized to throw off years of training in knowing their place and build self-confidence so that they reject their oppressor's definition of them.[11]

Both of these conditions have been met. The recent popularity and rapid growth of a singles subculture has been more visible in urban settings. Over 60 percent of all single persons live in cities.[12] This growing acceptance of singleness in society was instrumental in my own resocialization process.

> When I moved to Chicago in 1970 and lived on the near-north side in singleland, singleness was the "in-thing." The irony of it all was that when I returned to live in a Mennonite community and work in a Mennonite institution, I began to understand for the first time what singles were really feeling when they described alienation. This experience made me feel as if I wanted to flee to the city and join others who found affirmation of their singleness outside the church.

I believe that the church too often follows on the heels of society, when it should be a leader in resocializing persons. Resocialization means a more basic and rapid change, especially it means leaving one way of life for another that is not only different from the former but incompatible with it.[13] For example, when a "sinner" is converted to a religious way of life that person is being resocialized.

In order to consider the possibility of the church assuming the role of a resocialization agent, in regard to singleness, two questions must be examined. What are the beliefs of the church, and what are the consequences of those beliefs?

> One day while having coffee with two ministers, one of

them warned me, "When you write your chapter for your book on singleness, don't quote the apostle Paul. He says that every Christian should consider singleness so that they have more time to devote to the kingdom of God. I think singles who remain single become selfish." While I had to agree that not all singles use their singleness to an advantage in Christ's work, that comment made me question whether our cultural presuppositions interpret Scripture.

The Christian church tends to disregard Christ and the apostle Paul on the issue of singleness. Too often we place so much emphasis on the issue of Christ's divinity that we sometimes do not take him seriously as a model. Furthermore, Christ not only broke with the Jewish tradition which required marriage, he broke with any structure which singles out people and promotes injustice.

Too many theologians have said that the apostle Paul is biased against marriage and that his opinion does not count, David Schroeder observes. But that is a misunderstanding of Paul; Paul is saying that Christians do have a choice. Schroeder says, "It is Christian to remain single as well as marry, and the option to remain single should be an option open to all Christians." He concludes that it is time for the church to stop feeling sorry for singles and to stop seeing them as unfortunate and unfulfilled persons in society.[14]

Other theologians and sociologists argue that, although Christians clearly believe the New Testament moves beyond the Old, they ignore the documents in the New Testament regarding singleness. For example, J. Howard Kauffman, in his description of the Mennonite family, indicates that Mennonites fortify the family institution with a literal interpretation of Scriptures. He goes on to say:

> Mennonites believe in the words of God when he said con-

> cerning Adam, "It is not good for man to be alone" (Gen. 2:18). Considerable social pressure is normally exerted against the bachelor and "old maid." With regard to size of family, Mennonites tend to accept literally God's command to Noah, "Be fruitful and multiply, and replenish the earth."[15]

Kauffman cites the history of more than 400 years of agrarian living as contributing to this emphasis on marriage and procreation.

What are the consequences of the church's failure to develop a belief for singleness? The major consequences are the stereotyping of singles, myths regarding both singleness and marriage, and lack of guidance on how to discern God's will and guidance on physical intimacy.

Too often singles feel that marriage is the answer to all their problems because they have not heard married persons talk about their struggles. As Bertha Beachy, a single, says, "Married persons seem to adopt either one of two myths about single persons—they are to be pitied or envied."[16] While I never thought of myself as being the object of pity, I certainly have had women tell me over and over again, "You are so lucky you are single. I did not have a choice. Don't marry."

Another common myth is that singles are not whole persons. This is a common myth in spite of Christ's definition of wholeness, as being relationships, not marriage. Christ honored marriage, but did not equate it with wholeness.

> Several years ago, I was on my way to give a lecture entitled "Being Single and Whole." One of my colleagues looked at the poster advertising this and said, "I did not think it was possible to be single and whole." When I questioned him as to what he meant, he said society does not think it is possi-

ble. Then he went on to say that it was regarded as a shame to have "old maids" in the family, so he tried hard to marry his sisters off. At that moment I wanted to respond, "Is that why you now feel such a responsibility to marry off your brothers and sisters in the community of believers?"

Through its emphasis on marriage, the church also gives mixed messages on sexual expression. Ruth Krall, a single, said at a conference on sexuality in 1980, "If you believe that sexual intercourse is necessary to create wholeness of person, then the single person who seeks to be whole by definition needs to seek sexual intercourse."[17] Her presentation sparked a lot of discussion on the conflicting sexual messages singles receive from the church. The younger singles said they frequently receive the message "wait," while the "older" singles said they receive the command "don't." In the absence of clear guidance from the church, some singles are influenced by the sexual mores of our society. The group concluded that it is difficult for the church to develop guidelines for either persons of homosexual or heterosexual orientation, without first developing a theology of human sexuality.

Because you and I comprise the church, we have the power to turn everything around. Not only can we begin to resocialize persons by reshaping values and attitudes toward singleness, we can begin to socialize children so that they are better prepared for the possibility of singleness and develop positive self-images, which will not be dependent on their marital state.

We are not saying that socialization and resocialization would result in a sudden and dramatic change. Our churches and their schools are steeped in tradition, and it would take task forces to work on developing curriculum which would not leave out or stereotype singles. However, on the positive side, our religious teachings provide models. What are these models? First, the Christian vision stresses the transformation of the entire way of the individual believer and of society so that it should be fashioned after the teachings and example of Christ. As stated previously, Christ not only broke with any structures that oppress or single out any group of people, he broke with the cultural norm and remained single. Also, the Christians have attempted to pattern church life after the New Testament church.

Mennonites did follow the tradition of the early church in honoring singles; only women were appointed to be congregational deacons because it was thought the gifts required were more suitable for women. The *Dordrecht Confession* in 1632, Article IX, cites 1 Timothy 5:9, Romans 16:1, and James 1:27 as the basis for electing "honorable" widows to the office of deaconess in the church. In 1944 the *Mennonite Church Polity* manual also cites 1 Timothy 5:9-10 as the basis for electing honorable widows. The manual states that a sister, usually the wife of a deacon, could be assigned deaconess duties.[18] The trend currently is to select a deaconess on the basis of her gifts rather than her marital or widowed status.

In the General Conference Mennonite Church, single women could elect to join the deaconess movement of the 19th century—a kind of Protestant religious order.[19] The vision of this movement was that these sisters would be involved in community outreach or be missionaries within their "home turf." Unfortunately, the primary image came to be that of a nurse, since a nurse's training program and institutions requiring the services of a nurse had been established at the beginning specifically to implement this type of diaconate.

These deaconesses were referred to as sisters and lived together for the purpose of spiritual support, but they were not cloistered like Roman Catholic orders. Furthermore, like other Protestant diaconates, their ordination did not include a pledge to celibacy. These women were put on their honor in this regard, since they had to pledge themselves to the Lord to be "free from all other duties" in order to devote their time and effort to the service of the Lord in ministering to suffering humanity.[20]

Not surprisingly only a handful of sisters were present among us, because lifetime commitment and a restrictive ordered life did not keep pace with our changing times.

What kind of an adaptation of the deaconess program could be implemented? We could capture the value of living in covenanted community. Some singles have already discovered that possibility. We could recapture the idea of commissioning persons who decide they could serve God better as a single. We could include men as well and develop a kind of dispersed order in keeping with our highly mobile society. Or we could provide support groups.

The crucial question is, what do singles need? While each single is a unique being, there are some commonalities. The greatest need single people feel in leaving the traditional family structure is to have substitute networks of human relationships. These networks can help fulfill the basic needs of intimacy, sharing, and continuity. Art Gish states "Community can provide them [single people] with a broad network of supportive relationships, lessening the feeling that they simply must marry, and give them a better basis on which to make decisions regarding marriage."[21]

Lois Barrett, a writer and editor, describes the possibilities the New Testament church has in terms of meeting singles' needs.

> There is one form of family which is to model Jesus' love above all other—the church. The early church after Pentecost resembled a family in many ways; its members ate together, shared possessions, prayed together in each other's homes. They came to regard each other as brothers and sisters.
>
> The church is a family in which no one need feel left out—those who have never married, those whose families have died or have left them, those who do not share the same beliefs as their biological families.[22]

This excerpt, which is based on an Acts passage (see Acts 2:42-47), identifies Koinonia as a critical factor in becoming the family of God. John Driver, in his book, *Becoming God's Community*, elaborates on the community of Koinonia. He says:

> It means spiritual as well as material sharing. Its usage in the New Testament makes it clear that Koinonia means sharing a common life within the body of Christ at all levels—spiritual, social, intellectual, and economic. No area of life is excluded.[23]

A popular adaptation of this model has been the division of the congregation into house churches or small groups commonly referred to as Koinonia groups. This kind of group could provide a caring atmosphere with a high level of trust, where both singles and married persons could share their struggles and give to each other. For example, singles could discuss concerns such as sexuality and how to determine if God wants them to remain single or marry. The possibilities for mutual aid and emotional support are endless. For example, parents often welcome relief from the intense demands of children, while some singles love to relate to children. Various books are available to give some practical guidance on how to divide the church into households of God.[24]

If we take Koinonia seriously, we will not follow the individualism of Western society where each household does its own thing. Some singles do not feel the need for a small group, because the Sunday school setting may result in the same kind of sharing. My own experience has been that I experienced the meaning of Koinonia in some Sunday school classes, whereas some small groups, like the larger church, were geared to couples.

Other helpful structures within the church have been the retreats sponsored for singles. While some have objected to such retreats because they exclude marrieds, any group that has been oppressed needs to be brought together and resocialized by healing wounds so that it can begin to feel okay. Then, these singles can sponsor weekends within the church, where married and single persons can work at breaking down the barriers and becoming the family of God.

Not only do singles need married persons; married persons also need singles. We need each other. Gifts of the spirit are needed for community expression and the diversity among us coupled with God's gift to the church—the gift of the spirit can result in becoming the family of God. Brothers and sisters, let us join together and become the family which God intended us to be.

Notes

1. Information in a memo to the author from Vernon Jantzi, professor at Eastern Mennonite College, October 14, 1981.

2. John Christian Wenger, ed., *The Complete Works of Menno Simons* (Scottdale, Pa.: Herald Press, 1956), p. 250.

3. Walter Klaassen, ed., *Anabaptism in Outline* (Scottdale, Pa.: Herald Press, 1981), p. 228.

4. Edward S. Morgan, *The Puritan Family* (New York: Harper and Row, (1966), pp. 145-146, cited in Keith Melville, ed., *Marriage and Family* (New York: Random House, 1977), p. 122.

5. J. William Frost, *The Quaker Family in Colonial America* (New York: St. Martin's Press, 1973), p. 150.

6. Jantzi, *op. cit.*

7. Sherry Andrews, "Why Is the Church Becoming Single-Minded," *Charisma* (May 1981), p. 33.

8. Peter J. Stein, ed., *Single Life: Unmarried Adults in Social Context* (New York: St. Martin's Press, 1981), p. 13.

9. Jantzi, *op. cit.*

10. Peter J. Stein, "Singlehood: An Alternative to Marriage," in Kenneth C. W. Kammeyer, ed., *Confronting the Issues: Marriage, the Family, and Sex Roles*, 2nd ed. (Boston: Allyn and Bacon, 1981), p. 36.

11. J. Victor Baldridge, *Sociology a Critical Approach to Power, Conflict, and Change*, 2nd ed. (New York: John Wiley and Sons, 1980), p. 518.

12. Carter, H., and P. C. Glick, *Marriage and Divorce: A Social and Economic Study* (Cambridge, Mass.: Harvard University Press, 1976), cited in Stein, *op. cit.*, p. 13.

13. Leonard Broom and Philip Selznick, *Essentials of Sociology* (New York: Harper and Row, 1979), p. 100.

14. David Schroeder, "Theology of Singleness," lecture presented at Laurelville Mennonite Church Center, Laurelville, Pa., July 5, 1977.

15. J. Howard Kauffman, "Family," in *The Mennonite Encyclopedia* (Scottdale, Pa.: Mennonite Publishing House; Newton, Kan.: Mennonite Publication Office; Hillsboro, Kan.: Mennonite Brethren Publishing House), 2nd printing, 1972, p. 295.

16. Bertha Beachy, Panel Discussion on Singleness, Akron Mennonite Church, Akron, Pa., February, 1978.

17. Ruth E. Krall, "Sexual Perspectives: Expressions of Femaleness and Maleness," lecture presented at Laurelville Mennonite Church Center, Laurelville, Pa., May 24, 1980.

18. Mennonite General Conference Church Polity Committee, *Mennonite Church Polity* (Scottdale, Pa.: Herald Press, 1944), pp. 24, 53.

19. Lois Barrett, "Looking at the Deaconess Movement Again," *The Mennonite*, Vol. 91 (January 20, 1976), p. 48.

20. Bethel Deaconess Home and Hospital (The Board of Directors of the Bethel Deaconess Home and Hospital Society, 1918), p. 19.

21. Art Gish, *Living in Christian Community* (Scottdale, Pa.: Herald Press, 1979), p. 88.

22. Lois Barrett, "Who Is My Family?" *The Mennonite*, Vol. 92 (June 7, 1977), p. 384.

23. John Driver, *Becoming God's Community* (Elgin, Ill.: The Brethren Press; Nappanee, Ind.: Evangel Press; Newton, Kan.: Faith and Life Press; Scottdale, Pa.: Mennonite Publishing House, 1981), p. 54.

24. An example would be Paul M. Miller, *Leading the Family of God* (Scottdale, Pa.: Herald Press, 1981).

Chapter 4

Singleness and Scripture

Bible Stories for Singles
By Lois Janzen

Ten years ago I was struggling with the fact that my congregation was 99 percent married people. The single people over age 24 had almost nothing in common except that we were single and there was no real place in the congregation for us. I felt out of place. Since my father was also my pastor, I was telling dad how I felt. In the discussion, dad remarked that he viewed single people to be in the biblical category of "widows and orphans" and the New Testament church had been given special injunction to care for such people. I was intensely angry with this remark, and I left in tears—much to his bafflement and amazement, for he had not meant to say anything to hurt me. From his point of view, he was simply stating a fact of classification that had no emotional valuation to it—much like the process of sorting silverware to go in the drawer. So why was I so mad?

At the time, I understood two things. I resented the paternalism, the assumption that he was okay, but that I needed help. That what was for me a daily fact of my existence should be looked upon as somehow abnormal requiring special responses from people made me angry. I disdained the formation of singles groups within the congregation because I wanted more than anything else to be in the mainstream. I did not want to be stuck off in some marginal group of which the others would occasionally have to remind themselves—"Oh yeah, we've got to consider what they want."

On the other hand, I also understood that I was somehow distinguishing myself from both groups of people, those in the mainstream and the widows and orphans. And I agreed that the latter were among the wounded of the congregation. But I, among the wounded? I felt strong and, for the most part, liked being single. I couldn't understand making a big point that singleness was a wound so I didn't want to join up with the "widows and the orphans." And yet our conversation had begun with me complaining because my needs weren't being met! So after I cried, I had to laugh for here was a major contradiction: I believed I was whole, not especially lacking anything, that I had lots to give *and* that I was not whole, I was lacking much that others had, that I needed gifts too.

Since then I've learned that other contradictions were feeding this basic one: I would simultaneously ask for help and then refuse it; I had continued to think of myself as a child but everybody else was an adult; I both loved and hated being a woman; I equated adulthood with marriage and the love of a good man and yet wanted to prove that it was possible to be adult without either! All of these contradictions did produce wounds, and more and more, without any prodding from anybody, I finally began to think I was poor orphan Annie!

All those people whose company I had disdained before began to be interesting. How did people deal with the difficulties in their lives? Some, I noticed, responded with courage and joy; others continued to complain. I determined to stop complaining. But to do that I needed to fully accept both sides of that first, basic contradiction: I am whole, I am not whole.

In what has become a still unfinished journey toward acceptance, I discovered that the Bible does not say a great deal about being single as such. You will find no chapters telling you how to get over your uneasiness at eating alone in a restaurant, how to feel comfortable at a party of mostly married people, how to conquer loneliness, or how to improve your self-image. The thrust of the Scriptures do help, however, to broaden the limited definitions of wholeness based on restricting parental and societal expectations and on childhood perceptions to pictures of wholeness which enable creative living. Moreover, the Scriptures are quite helpful in telling with honesty the stories of a whole host of people who also carried within them the same contradiction I continue to experience: I am whole; I am not whole.

What follows, then, is an outline of the creation story because that story provides at least three major affirmations of the "I am whole" side of things. The claims put forth are that our lives are a gift of grace, each person is a whole person, and everyone has a vocation, a reason for being in the world. To illustrate the first and third points I have included the stories of persons experiencing the "I am not whole" side. I must emphasize that this chapter is not a systematic account of all that the Bible says on the subject of wholeness; it is more an illustration of recurring biblical themes.

In the first chapters of Genesis, the Bible calls us to establish our identities in God. Genesis 1:26-27 make it clear that our lives are God's idea in the first place; none of us asked to be born. Each of our lives is a gift of love, and in a fundamental, foundational sense, most of us exist because somebody else wanted us to. In the beginning, God made it possible for each of us to be.

If this seems like an obvious and clichéd point to be making, it is, nevertheless, the first point I forget when I am lonely, self-pitying, or feeling trapped. But a whole series of birth stories besides the creation story remind us that our lives come from God. For example, Sarah had long given up hope of a child. When God came to tell her she would have a child at 90 years of age, naturally she laughed. "What? At my age? You've got to be kidding!" God is offended at her laughter and asks her, "Is anything too hard for the Lord?" Sarah knows intellectually that the answer is supposed to be "No, nothing is too hard." But still, the idea of having a child at her age was awfully hard to fathom. The Lord gives her the son despite her skepticism. And she names the son, Isaac, or Laughter, because "God has made laughter for me." (For the full story, see Genesis 17, 18, and 21.)

We singles can identify with and learn from this story in two ways. First, just as Adam and Eve were God's idea, so was Isaac, and so were all of us. We were meant to be gifts of laughter to other people. We all regularly delighted our families when we were infants. Wholeness, therefore, in adult life is based on maintaining and renewing the awareness that our lives were and are a product of our parents' love, that life is a gift from God and that God's hope and our parents' hope were that we would be sources of delight, laughter, and comfort. This giftedness and this hope is the truth despite feelings and experiences that seem to say otherwise. Single persons need to base self-images and identities solidly on this fact.

The psalmist puts it this way:

> For thou didst form my inward parts,
> thou didst knit me together in my mother's womb.
> I praise thee, for thou art fearful and wonderful.
> Wonderful are thy works!
> Thou knowest me right well;
> my frame was not hidden from thee
> when I was being made in secret,
> intricately wrought in the depths of the earth.
>
> (Ps. 139:13-15, RSV)

Second, we singles can learn from Sarah's experience with God in looking at the difference between her attitude and God's attitude. Sarah had long ago made peace with having to be childless. She felt old, thought pleasure had long ago deserted her. And perhaps she felt that she no longer had the right to ask anything more of life than what it already had been. She was mostly letting time go by. God, however, had other ideas. New life, a different life, pleasure are always a possibility in God's mind; God wanted to give Sarah laughter.

I like God's treatment of Sarah. God did not dismiss her past dream of a child, although she nearly had. Nor was God content to let her sit in her routine of barrenness, disillusionment, and sarcasm. Sarah was challenged to move out of all that. Biblical wholeness is being honest about both past and present realities but then letting God start one off on some new track, even when it seems fairly ridiculous to do so. When one's identity and self-image are based on God's willingness to do the new thing, then creative single life is altogether possible. We can make the fresh start, and do the unexpected. "Is anything too hard for the Lord?"

Let's return to the creation story. Although this passage is often used to emphasize the sanctity of marriage, the interrelationship of male and female, the passage also suggests that both male and female are whole unique systems by themselves. Neither is a deficient work of creation. They each were created to be able to survive. Adam was quite busy with his task of subduing the earth, naming and taming the animals. Since he was getting along quite well, the creation of woman was not a matter of his survival! It was God who perceived that the man was lonely. Woman was God's idea and work, not Adam's. In fact, Adam is surprised and astonished when he wakes up to find woman there. Woman, too, was pronounced by God to be a good work so she is not deficient, either.

Consequently, solitariness need not be fundamentally destructive or necessarily a mark of non-wholeness. God had pronounced man to be a "very good" work. Adam's loneliness, it seems to me, came about because there was so much abundance, such a rich variety of life to experience. I imagine Adam yearning to share his awe and astonishment the first time he ever saw a hippopotamus. Perhaps he got stuck over what to call those bothersome insects we now know as cockroaches and wished he could brainstorm with somebody over a proper name for them! At least one of the great blessings another person provides is an occasion to express the joy inside.

An important developmental task for singles is to discover that one's loneliness is not a defect but a sign and a gift of life. Solitude, properly spent, helps one maintain a grateful surprise at how much one's needs are indeed met. And at the same time, solitude surprises one into learning how many others there are who are "bone of my bones and flesh of my flesh."

Third, the creation story says that everyone has been given a vocation, a task, a reason for being in the world. Specifically, it says, "Be fruitful and multiply, fill the earth and subdue it." Wholeness involves fulfilling this command. Also, the word "subdue" suggests that a struggle will be involved in the accomplishing of this task. This means that a definition of wholeness must include the presence of obstacles. Moreover, if one reads this text in the light of Jesus, the struggle to fill the earth must mean more than having children as Jesus often used the imagery of "being fruitful" in contexts that were not simply biological. (See the parable of the sower, Mark 4, or Jesus' attitudes toward trees that bear fruit.) Fruitfulness, as Jesus uses it, always means being properly rooted in the Word of God and then using power to act on the Word. The quest to be fruitful, in other words, involves getting to know God better so that one can give life to others. Being fruitful is a lifelong vocation that does not exempt one from pain or necessarily produce happiness in the sense that all one's needs get met. Jesus' attempt to be fruitful brought him out of the desert solitude into the busy cities and towns and eventually took him to the cross. Early in his ministry he indicated that to follow him one had to leave father and mother behind; although he respected people's biological loyalties and interests, his own creative task moved him beyond his own survival and family clan.

An Old Testament illustration of a single person who exemplified wholeness in a situation where family loyalty and biological fruitfulness were called into question is found in Judges 11. This chapter tells how Jephthah, judge of Israel, is involved in a war with the Ammonites. The battles are not going well, and in desperation, he prays a vow to God to sacrifice whoever comes out to meet him on his return home if the Lord would give him victory over the Ammonites. The Lord does give victory, but when he returns home, his only child and daughter comes dancing out the door to meet him. Jephthah, in terrible grief, tells his daughter about the vow he made. He says that he feels he cannot go back on it. She agrees but asks for two months to go with her friends to the mountains "to bewail her virginity." Jephthah grants her that time, and then the Scripture reports in stark simplicity, "And at the end of two months, she returned to her father who did with her according to the vow which he had made."

Upon first reading this story, I found it horrible. It is very difficult to understand how the father had enough will power to carry out his vow. Why didn't he just laugh when he saw his daughter and realize that he had prayed a very foolish prayer? In contrast, the daughter's request "to bewail her virginity" shows extraordinary self-awareness on her part. These people seem extreme and a little unreal. How can we identify with them? Where is wholeness in this story? Jephthah's understanding of God seems lamentably incomplete; the submission of the daughter unnecessarily tragic.

However, upon second and third reading, this story can become an important story for singles. It raises the questions of what contribution to a community means and of what love is. It demonstrates two people taking seriously their commitment to God, taking responsibility for their actions, and making choices. It addresses the mourning involved in facing unlived life, unrealized possibilities.

By asking for time to bewail her virginity, the daughter was buying time to think through these issues in order to make it possible for her to freely walk to the altar of sacrifice. The options she had all involved death in some way: (1) she could refuse to comply with the vow, run away from home, live with a break in the relationship with her father; (2) she could comply but unwillingly and insure a dreadful scene on the day of sacrifice, for at the last moment her body would draw back if she were not fully united in heart and mind; (3) she could submit and do so joyfully.

Not only did she need time to consider her options, she needed time to get past the notion that procreation is the only way to contribute to the larger community. In ancient Israel, woman's highest calling was to get married and bear sons. Children were the realization of the promise to Abraham: "I will make you the father of nations." If she was not going to marry and have children, what was the reason for her being born? What had been her contribution to life so far? Once she had answered that question, there was the fear that "If I die now, what will remain of me?" In other words, she needed time to affirm that although she had not done all that could have been done, she had lived well, even so. And she needed to know that something of her life would continue on in the lives of her friends who would spend that time with her.

Negatively, she needed to grieve for all she would miss. She needed time to forgive her father's foolish vow, to understand why it was necessary. She needed a deep certainty that she would die for him because she understood and respected his love for God, his position of leadership in Israel.

Contrary then to my first thought, I find a sense of wholeness in this story. Consider this woman's integrity! She did not withdraw her love for her father, nor did she deny concern for herself. Wholly and spontaneously present, she shows us glimpses of a vibrant personality: at first dancing and laughing joyously, then crying, facing options, loving her friends, taking strength and courage from the mountain retreat.

The story makes a point that though she had not sexually united with one man, she had, nevertheless, come to belong to the whole community, particularly to the women who commemorated her life and death four times a year. To them, it was clear that she had loved deeply and wholeheartedly, and therefore deserved to be remembered. She was special.

Jephthah's daughter concluded that love was her reason for being; in her case, this love was for her father. And like Jesus, her love moved her beyond cultural expectations. Don't misunderstand; I am not saying that singles must live martyred lives. But I do think freedom and wholeness involve the courage to let go. And letting go involves a death of some sort. Letting go is different for each person. Some may need to let go of the workaholic, success-oriented side in order to discover the delights of lazy time with a friend. Or, it may mean letting go of one's attachments at home in order to establish a life of one's own. Or, it may mean revising one's assumptions about how to spend one's time in order to be a more giving person.

The mourning time begins this letting-go process. If we allow ourselves the time to really mourn whatever feels unlived, unrealized, not whole, when we pass through the other side, we can discover a very deep affirmation of life. And even though we don't have it all, what we have is very good. Curiously enough, experiencing fully both aspects of wholeness and non-wholeness often give one the strength to do something about the non-whole side.

Because Paul knew so well how his response to the living Lord had changed his life, had given it purpose and meaning, had taken him through all sorts of wild adventures, he could advise the people in Corinth asking about singleness and marriage (and I'm paraphrasing 1 Corinthians 7:24, 32), "Well, whichever you are, don't worry about it!"

Paul's remarks in 1 Corinthians 7 often fall on puzzled

ears because we know ourselves to be worrying, and it seems like a flippant dismissal of our worry. But Paul is right. For when we are ready to assent that the Lord is very good, that our life is good, and that its whole point is to be loving God with all our hearts, souls, and minds, and our neighbors as ourselves, then the fruitfulness and the multiplication that Genesis 1 speaks of is realized. Life is whole because it is God's.

Chapter 5

Singleness and Sexuality

A Gift from God

By Martha Smith Good

The question "How do you as a single person cope with your sexual needs?" came quite unexpectedly. Although we had been close friends for a long time, our conversations had never touched this intimate topic. Because of our firm friendship I realized this was more than a casual, curious question. Was I free enough to share my experience? Gradually we relaxed, as both husband and wife and I talked about our common gift—sexuality—and how we, whether single or married, accept that gift and integrate it into our total being. This conversation was a beginning recognition point that a need exists for open communication among persons on a topic affecting every human being: sexuality. This chapter seeks to explore sexuality from the belief that all persons, created in the image of God, are sexual beings, capable of, and indeed called to be in fellowship with each other as male and female.

Our Creator God has given to us many unique gifts. One of the gifts is sexuality. Sexuality—being either male or female—has been conferred by God onto each individual.

How we claim and use such a beautiful gift determines our freedom to let it become a gift to others. The gift of sexuality, when adequately integrated into our total personality, allows us to move beyond ourselves into vital relationships with others, which provide a seedbed for mutual spiritual, emotional, and psychological growth. The acceptance of this gift is enhanced by taking a new look at ourselves as sexual beings created for relationships and by seeing the distinctions between "sex" and our sexuality.

We are created for relationships. The basic theme of the Genesis stories of creation is *God's love* for his people. God's concern, as he looked out over his creation, was man's struggle with loneliness and lack of fellowship. Among all the animals God created was none that could meet the human need for companionship. Because God never intended for anyone to live in isolation and loneliness he created a counterpart who would provide the needed fellowship in a complementary manner. Now God's image was complete. When God brings woman to man she is accepted as his partner and the completion of his humanness. As the two come together, the maleness and femaleness of each is recognized, and they affirm their complementarity without shame.

Human sexuality is best understood within the framework of the theology of creation. That is, God created us to be in fellowship with himself and with each other. It was an intentional act of God to create us sexual beings. When we see the creation account as the basis for human fellowship and interaction between the sexes, we are free to affirm sexuality as a good thing. Acknowledging sexuality as a God-given gift enables us to develop as mature persons. Further, this view recognizes sexuality as an avenue for depth relationships in fellowship and unity among men and women.

When this understanding is accepted, all persons,

whether single or married, are seen as sexual beings. It affirms sexuality as God's gift to all persons created in his image and it affirms God's intent for male and female fellowship in various forms of relationship. Finally, and perhaps most significantly, this understanding recognizes that all of God's people, single and married, need each other.

We are created as sexual beings. The Genesis accounts of creation tell us that *both* male and female are created in the image of God. God's image is most accurately reflected in the combined fellowship and interaction of male and female. When viewing sexuality from the framework of being created in God's image, it becomes necessary to distinguish between male and female reflecting the image of God as they interact in Christian fellowship, and male and female relating to each other within the institution of marriage. The marriage relationship may or may not reflect this image, depending upon the freedom, fidelity, and mutuality between the two partners. Too often sexuality has been seen only within the context of marriage, an idea which has dominated our attitudes in the past. When all persons are accepted as sexual beings, however, persons outside of a marriage relationship can be included with ease in male and female fellowship as sexual beings created in the image of God.

The traditional way of understanding the male and female distinction within the framework of the marriage institution is a reversal of what was intended by God in creating us in his image.[1] What needs to take precedence, as we study sexuality, is a new look toward understanding male and female relatedness in fellowship with each other and with God. This argument asserts that a life without marriage *does* have the freedom to experience the fellowship of male and female in the image of God. No one can be male or female in the abstract. We are male or female as we encounter the opposite sex. In this encounter, as pictured in Genesis 2, we experience more completely our sexuality and therefore what it means to be fully created in the image of God.

One can further assert that theology of man (humankind) must see the man and woman relationship as central.[2] If we recognize this as a fundamental principle then we can see and affirm the existence of the male/female relationship outside of the marriage institution. The marriage relationship exists then, as only one form of a complex human fellowship and perhaps not even the most basic. The most basic consists of a male-female fellowship expressing itself in a variety of relationships, each of which is beneficial both to the individual and to society as a whole.[3] A group of persons composed of married and single men and women that is committed to meet regularly for discussion, fellowship, caring, and sharing provides a climate in which a variety of relationships may exist. Within this context the individual gives and receives, nourishes, and is nourished. Thus the person's contact with the larger society has a quality of depth that reflects mature awareness and appreciation of self and others.

When we dare to agree with this view our perspective on human sexuality broadens. For it is then that sexuality becomes more than its physical elements. Within this framework human sexuality moves far beyond the desire for physical sexual expression. We have tended to take the attitude that "sexuality is sex." Human sexuality does not exist only within marriage. Sexuality does not necessarily mean physical sexual pairing. Paul Jewett claims that "the Christian view of human sexuality is not all one and the same with the Christian view of marriage."[4] They are not the same. Herein lies a solution to the singles' dilemma of how they dare recognize and affirm their own sexuality. Herein lies also a new awareness for married persons who believe sexuality is common to and expressed only within the marriage relationship.

For the sake of clarity it is crucial to make a definitive distinction between sex and sexuality. Although they are closely related, they are not to be seen as one and the same.

Sex is a biologically based need. It is oriented not only toward procreation, but also toward pleasure and tension release. It aims at genital activity that ends in orgasm. Although sex usually includes a variety of human and religious meanings, the focus is upon erotic activities largely of a genital nature.

Sexuality, on the other hand, is a much more comprehensive definition. Although it includes sex and relates to biological organ systems, sexuality goes beyond the physical.

Sexuality is not the whole of one's personality, but it is a very basic dimension of our personhood. While our sexuality does not determine all of our feelings, thoughts, and actions, in many ways it touches and affects them all. Sexuality is our self-understanding and way of being in the world as male and female. It includes our development of attitudes and characteristics which have been culturally defined as masculine or feminine. It includes our feelings toward those of the opposite and/or the same sex. It includes our attitudes about our bodies and those of others. Because we are "bodyselves" our sexuality constantly reminds each of us of our uniqueness and particularity. We look different and we feel different from any other person. Sexuality is a sign, a symbol, and a means of our call to communication and communion.

The mystery of sexuality is the mystery of our need to reach out and embrace others both physically and spiritually. Sexuality thus expresses God's intention that we find our authentic humanness in relationship. But such humanizing cannot occur in the human way alone. Sexuality, we must say, is tied in with our relationship with God.[5]

There is a distinction between "affective" sexuality, and "genital" sexuality.[6] Affective sexuality embodies the spiritual, emotional, and psychological aspects of our humanness. Affective sexuality reaches out to include the whole area of emotional warmth given only to those created in the image of God. In essence, it is the totality of all that we are as we express ourselves, individually and corporately, in our relatedness as male and female in friendship and in fellowship.

Genital sexuality refers to the physiological coming together of male and female in sexual intercourse. This emphasis focuses on the sensuous, erotic, pleasurable act of physical sexual activity. Genital sexuality includes also the awareness and affirmation of the physical sex drive crying out for bodily fulfillment and satisfaction. Unfortunately, the genital aspect often emerges as the central understanding of sexuality.

One of the fallacies in our understanding of sexuality has been this overemphasis on genital sex. This one small area of a larger, more complete whole has had to bear the full weight of defining sexuality. Two disastrous results have followed. One has been an assumption that only those in a marriage relationship may be sexual beings because they have the freedom to engage in sexual intercourse. The single individual who has no freedom for genital sexual expression has become, as it were, a non-sexual being. However, the single individual who has had the opportunity to face the reality of discovering affective sexuality experientially may be as sexually mature, if not more so, than the person in a marriage relationship where sexuality as genital sex is taken for granted. Single persons who can freely and comfortably respond to both males and females with love, gentleness, and compassion are most likely in touch with their affective sexuality. This in no way implies an absence of genital feelings. It does suggest, though, that these persons have acquired a broad understanding of sexuality and recognize that genital sex is not the only means of sexual expression.

The other consequence of reducing sexuality to sex has been to repress these normal physical genital feelings when there has been no marital bond in which to achieve a sexual climax. Repression only serves to intensify the desire and urge for sexual intercourse. When these strong feelings predominate and are seen as "bad" it is impossible to get in touch with the affective dimension of sexuality. What is needed is a new freedom to feel our genital desires and urgings and to affirm our okayness in being who we are.

The freedom to accept and affirm the physical drives and to feel comfortable with their presence even though unexpressed moves us toward greater wholeness. Genital sexual feelings are beautiful. They move us on to recognize the additional dimension of affective sexual feelings. It is more than coincidence that we associate sexuality with love. It is God's design that this strong physical drive be meshed with our ability to love and care. Genital and affective sexuality are mysteriously intertwined. Each is to be claimed with gratitude as a unique divine gift to be used wisely, discreetly and with integrity in male and female relationships.

As God's creatures we have been created with a unique set of checks and balances. We are given minds to think, to plan, to wonder, and we were also given strong emotions which cry out from deep within us for expression and gratification. The two, mind and emotions, create an inner tension early in life. A child may wish to cry when hurt and yet the mind has picked up the message that it is wrong to cry. The tension, in this case, between desire and acceptable behavior may be intense and thus confusing. The first awareness of an additional tension (sexual awakening) presents itself in the early teen years. It is then that we begin to search for a balance between our minds—what we know—and our bodies—what we feel. As we become older the balance becomes more a part of us, but the tension between the two continues to exist.

The gift of sexuality presents itself to us in the form of inner restlessness, a strong desire to be loved, and also a very direct sexual desire for physical intimacy. The struggle during adolescence and into adulthood is "what to do with all of this." For many persons this struggle is never talked about openly. The sexual revolution of the previous decade resolved the issue by strongly advocating free sexual expression in intercourse as a means of coming to terms with one's sexuality. This, however, tended to separate sex even further from the broader, personal nature of sexuality.

The church's silence on sexuality has often forced youth, singles, and other adults to adopt their understanding of sexuality and its development from society. This pattern can be broken by taking to heart a theology of creation that affirms sexuality and letting go of sexuality narrowly defined as sex. The church must assert herself in teaching what it means to be created in the image of God. The subsequent implications of that belief then become practical in wholesome male-female interaction. Such relationships have integrity when they affirm the sexuality of all persons.

The kind of attitude we develop toward sexuality is determined by whether we see our sexuality (1) as a threat, (2) an irresolvable tension relieved only through intercourse, (3) a strong uncontrollable force subject to explode, or (4) a gift which when properly directed becomes a beautiful expression of who we are as persons. Our God-given gift of sexuality is at the very base of who we are as loving persons.

Coming to terms with the differences between affective sexuality and genital sexuality leads to greater comfortableness with ourselves, with persons of the opposite sex, and with members of our same sex. Both coexist and are understood as distinctive in their own right. Both are recognized for the part they play in our becoming a whole person.

Intimacy has many different levels of social interaction. Intimacy with another person may be experienced emotionally, psychologically, spiritually, and physically. Physical intimacy is not necessarily at the head of the list, although it has too frequently been placed there.

When we view sexuality from the standpoint that we are sexual beings created in the image of God, then the spiritual, emotional, and psychological aspects of intimacy must take precedence over the physical. It is within the realm of these three that fellowship and unity in relation to God and each other can occur. God created man and woman for intimate fellowship, of which the physical is a part, but not the most basic or most important. We all need and desire spiritual and emotional intimacy. Sometimes this need may get confused with the sexual desire for physical expression. It is of crucial importance to see the difference. "Sex" as an attempt to find intimacy will only lead to hurt and confusion and will heighten the physical desire for more and more. Friendship does not imply the need for genital interaction.

Finally, we will survey sexual expression in Christian community. How God's love is experienced depends largely on how we, his people, express our love to each other. How we express our love to each other is determined by our understanding of what it means to be created in the image of God. To be in the image of God does not mean that we fully embody all the attributes we ascribe to God. Far from it! However, it does mean that God has given us the ability to be in relationship with each other as he is in relationship with us. Within the framework of the church we seek to relate in love in the emotional, spiritual, and psychological realms. In the Christian community our understanding of human relatedness sees Jesus as the principle role model for our behavior. Jesus, in his humanness, attempted to reveal to us more fully the nature of God's love as he moved among people leading them to greater wholeness. Jesus, then, becomes our model as we establish guidelines and principles for sexual expression in the context of the Christian community.

What kind of example was Jesus? We have no indication how concerned Jesus was about human sexuality, but we recognize that in his humanness Jesus was a sexual person. In case that seems to be a radical statement, permit me to clarify. If we see sexuality as that which draws us toward loving relationships and then is expressed as a deep care and concern for other persons, then we can also affirm the sexuality of Jesus. Jesus was a most tender, compassionate, loving person. Consider the story of the woman who poured expensive oil on Jesus' feet and dried them with her hair. A most sensuous act! Yet Jesus could accept her gift graciously and freely as her expression of love and gratitude for him. The story of Jesus, Mary, and Martha leads us to believe that Jesus had a very important relationship with these two women. In their home he sought refuge for himself and accepted their warm hospitality offered to him. Jesus freely offered gentleness, tenderness, compassion, and love. He likewise received them. Each one of these characteristics is a part of sexuality. Their integration into the total personality gives sexuality an affective dimension and includes all persons whether married or single.

The spiritual affective qualities of tenderness, gentleness, love, and compassion are to be sought as we seek to grow in our understanding of sexual maturity. These qualities grow out of a heart of love based on God's deep spiritual love for us. Nonmarital sexual relationships in the Christian context then become expressions of our experience in God's love and an affirmation of our belief that we are created in God's image and thus reflect the divine nature. Furthermore, because we are male or female these interactions are rightfully called sexual expressions. Such sexual expressions realize God's intention that there be depth male-female fellowship.

Our sexuality is our ability to care deeply about many people and develop quality relationships. Our sexuality is the ability to show love, warmth, tenderness, and affection in a genuine Christlike manner. It is a gift from God and therefore to be regarded as a valuable treasure.

Notes

1. This argument is made by Paul K. Jewett, *Man as Male and Female* (Grand Rapids: Eerdmans, 1975), p. 34.
2. Op. cit., p. 49.
3. Op. cit., p. 49.
4. Op. cit., p. 47.
5. These definitions are adapted from James B. Nelson, *Embodiment* (Minneapolis: Augsburg Publishing House, 1978), pp. 17-18.
6. See Donald Goergen, *The Sexual Celibate* (New York: Seabury Press, 1974), pp. 51-53.

Chapter 6

Singleness and the Church

Models for Singles Ministries

By Herta Funk

I believe in the church, that community of people gathered by God through Christ. We are called saints, believers, slaves, and servants, the people of God, the body of Christ, the new community, God's household and family. As Mark Lee has aptly said in "The Church and the Unmarried": "Paul did not visualize the church as a federation of families." Such exclusive focus on the family to the exclusion of single persons is foreign to the New Testament understanding of the church.

That is why I at times dare to be critical of the church. I love the family. Among other things, I have wanted to get Mennonite Marriage Encounter started and have taken Family Cluster leadership training. But I won't let the church forget that family-centeredness is not enough. Whether we like it or not, the single, widowed, divorced, and separated are among us. Sheer numbers, 55 million in the United States alone, should make us act. Remember: There is one single adult for every married couple in our society. Another way of looking at this, is that there are more than 60 million people in the U.S. between 18 and 38, half of whom are single. Their cause is not always popular. They are at times the forgotten people.

I confess that I used to be afraid to speak about singles in the church. Then one Sunday afternoon when I was talking to a single adult group a young father, divorced, with children, poured out his agony: "The weekends are the worst for me. I have my children to talk to. I can call a friend to talk about fishing. But beyond that there is no one with whom I can share on a deeper level. Sometimes I want to climb a wall." The experience led to a kind of conversion for me which resulted in determination to call the church to care about people like this young man.

It is not enough to know that single adults exist. The church can do some things. In six years of working in a marginal way with single adults I have found some ambivalence among them. They thoroughly enjoy events especially geared to their needs. On the other hand they fear ongoing programming that will once again isolate them from the mainstream of church life. Some young single adults feel odd in the church and would enjoy special programs for them. When they grow older they sometimes feel quite at home integrated into the total life of the church. It is therefore extremely important to make plans together with singles. Now for some suggestions.

1. *Know the single adults in your church.* Take a look at the church membership roll. How many single adults are there? Where are they? At universities, colleges, Bible schools, or trade schools? In jobs close to home? Is the group a stable or relatively transient group? What are the lines of communication binding the singles to the church? Do they attend worship services? Have they found a warm spot in some group like a young adult Sunday school class? Do they

stay away? Why do they stay away? Did they leave at a point of change or crisis, like a time of questioning their faith, or during a divorce or separation?

2. *Listen to single adults.* If you listen you will hear many of them say: I won't attend a "family" picnic, a "family" fun night, a "couples'" class, or—worse yet—a "pairs-and-spares" class. Don't think marriage is our only interest; stop your attempts at match-making; forget the old-maid and bachelor jokes. Don't worry about our being a threat to the family; we are not perpetual minors, mere half human beings, or unhappy individuals. We don't want to be considered a "problem" with which the church has to "deal." In other words, hang the stereotypes. Some single people may fit the above stereotypes. Most are as varied as any group of people.

3. *Plan as though single adults mattered.* Those who have experience in working with single adults advise that the pastor's support is crucial. If the pastor is sympathetic to the needs of single persons, something can happen. Because of the transiency of the young adult and singles population it is important to have some ongoing leadership to give stability to the programming. Most important of all, involve singles themselves in planning and in leadership. If they have responsible jobs during the work week they will be able to take initiative for their programs.

Britton Wood, author of *Single Adults Want to Be the Church, Too,* stumbled into single adult ministry because of his position as a campus minister. He realized that often singles, after leaving college, had no place to go in the church. That opened his eyes to other singles who were also neglected. People responded to the caring ministry which resulted. Yet more often what Canadian writer Margaret Clarkson says is true: "The church, which should be highly sensitive to human needs, is in many ways the hardest place for a single woman [or man] to find acceptance as a person."

Mark W. Lee in "The Church and the Unmarried" says: "Singles will need some activism. In the spirit of forbearance they need to apply appropriate pressure on the church ministry. They will succeed as they match their activism with creative and Christlike lives." It takes a great deal of courage for singles to stick with the church. One young single mother gave this advice to divorced Christians: "Act as if there is a place for you in the church, even if there isn't. A place will open." Not everyone is as courageous as my friend. Yet such action is a good antidote to the self-destructive attitude of self-pity or the tendency to blame others.

With this background on planning, I want to suggest some specific models for singles ministry.

1. *Young adult groups.* Of young adults, according to statistics, 26 percent attend church, even though 86 percent had some religious training in the past. That is true in spite of the fact that they are highly religious and very service-oriented. Writers on faith development, like John Westerhoff, say that many of them are in a "searching-faith" stage. One young adult asked: "Do you have a class for skeptics?" Does the church have a place where young adults can ask faith questions without posing a threat? "It is doubtful that singles will remain in a class which stifles discussion or prohibits the sharing of experiences," says Bobbie Reed in *Developing a Single Adult Ministry.* Many denominations, including Lutherans and Catholics, are devoting a great deal of attention to young adults and single adults.

2. *Studies for the congregation.* Some books on singleness lend themselves for congregational study. This book, in itself, is an attempt to provide such study. Another example is the collection of essays *It's O.K. to Be Single,* edited by Gary

R. Collins (Waco: Word Books, 1976). Some classes like to develop their own program so that they can draw on resources in the area. It is important to listen to what single persons themselves have to say.

3. *Books for the library.* At present many good books on singleness, divorce and remarriage, single parenting, stepparenting, and young adults are on the market. Each church should have a section available to its members. Those who have to make a sudden transition from married to single life would benefit from resources ranging from stages of grief to money management. The bibliography on page 81 lists many such books.

4. *Divorce recovery events.* The last retreat for formerly married which I conducted drew mostly young divorced persons. For the worship service, all picked up stones at the lake to represent their lives. One young man said of his piece of rock: "My stone is flat and round, with one part of the circle broken off. That is the way I felt when I came. But after this weekend I think I can begin to put the circle back together again." Few self-righteous Christians are among the divorced. Instead of condemnation they need affirmation. "Don't shoot, I'm already wounded," Jim Smoke advised the participants at a single adult leadership training (SALT I) event in 1980. People respond to a tough love which recognizes their hurt, yet challenges them to seek growth through the hard experiences.

5. *Help in stepparenting.* There are 11 million blended families in the United States. Dr. Thomas Holmes and colleagues at the University of Washington School of Medicine have developed a Social Readjustment Scale which gives points for 43 life events that can cause stress. An accumulation of 200 points may result in physical symptoms that indicate stress overload. A blended family with 5 step-

children can accumulate as many as 507 stress points. Those contemplating remarriage should be helped to understand the potential stresses of a stepfamily so that they can better prepare to face the challenges and minimize the stresses.

6. *Help for children of divorce.* Who helps children deal with divorce? One statistic shows that 65 percent of them think they were the cause of the divorce. Currently some good literature is available to help children understand what is happening. There is also some literature to help parents minimize this feeling of responsibility in their children.

7. *Single adult ministry as outreach.* Often people are open to the church at points of stress or crisis in their lives. One Mennonite church in the city advertises in the local paper that a single adult group is meeting for Bible study and sharing. People who would never enter the church otherwise come to share their distresses. This church discovered it is important to have good listeners, people who care, available to share the hurts of people. It also learned not to be discouraged because the group varied from week to week.

8. *Single-parenting assistance.* It is hard to be responsible for children every minute of the day and night. Single parents are so grateful if families in the church include their children in activities. Children need a number of adults as models. Because most single-parent families are headed by women, they are often poor. The *New York Times* (12-3-80) reported: "Women-led families are on the rise. Women now head 12 percent of all white families, 20 percent of all Hispanic families, and 41 percent of all black families. The median income in 1978 of women-led families was $8,540, less than half of the $17,640 median income of all families." Financial aid can at times minimize stresses. For instance, single parents may find it difficult to pay the registration fees

for special retreats, so the church could make scholarships available.

9. *Counseling services.* "We need to talk when grieving the death of a spouse or when agonizing through a divorce," says Bobbie Reed in *Developing a Single Adult Ministry.* "Sometimes we just need a person to listen and not respond. Sometimes we need an empathetic shoulder to cry on. Other times we are seeking specific guidance and counsel." The church could provide training in peer counseling to persons with sensitivity to the needs of others, yet who are able to refer serious problems to professionals.

10. *Service opportunities.* Research has shown that young adults are idealistic and service-oriented. It often takes someone in the church to lay a hand on a young single adult to consider voluntary service, missions, or the ministry. Some churches have discovered that young adults can be introduced to the challenges of Christian service during summer internships in the local church or through short-term service in North America or some foreign country. One Mennonite church which pays several of its young people minimum wage for church service rendered during the summer is seeing a number of them enter Christian service professions.

11. *Remarriage education.* The question of whether divorced persons should remarry is being discussed across the church. For some Christians remarriage is not an option. Many are, however, remarrying, and remarriage education is one way of standing with these people. Of all divorced persons, 80 percent remarry. Although 40 percent of first marriages fail, 60-70 percent of second marriages fail. Remarriage education, however, can bring down the failure rate the second time around. Such a program need not address the rightness or wrongness of remarriage, although

that question also needs to be addressed by the church.

And now for some do's and don'ts:

1. Do choose the direction for the involvement of single adults in the church in consultation with them.

2. Do make sure that singles groups have good support from the church. Offer leadership training if necessary. Remember: There is nothing which will hurt the church's credibility with singles as much as lukewarm commitment or shoddy programming.

3. Don't worry too much about success with numbers. It is a loving, caring framework which will not go out of style.

4. Do learn all you can from other churches, individuals with experience, and the young singles themselves to avoid the obvious pitfalls.

5. Do cooperate with other churches if your group is small. Sometimes it is crucial to expand the contacts of singles who have few social contacts.

6. Do strive for a balanced program of instruction, worship, fellowship, and service. In other words, don't compete with other organizations, but offer what the church does best.

7. Don't be discouraged by initial failure. Singles are often people in transition. Keep trying.

"Why do we need to single out singles?" asks Bobbie Reed. Her answer is: "We single out singles so that we can better minister to their unique needs."

In the final analysis the biblical axiom that it is not good for humans to be alone gives impetus to the inclusion of single persons in the church. James J. Lynch in his book, *The Broken Heart: The Medical Consequences of Loneliness*, documents that human relationships are vital to physical and emotional health. It is this love, friendship, and human contact which the church is eminently qualified to give.

Models for Singles Ministries / 81

The following bibliography is intended to provide program resources ministry with singles and young adults. For a broader listing of books see the general bibliography beginning on page 121.

The Church's Growing Edge: Single Adults. A Planning Guide. Published for Joint Educational Development by United Church Press, 132 West Thirty-first Street, New York, N.Y. 10001. A step-by-step guide on developing a ministry with single adults.

Gardner, Richard A. *The Boys and Girls Book About Divorce.* With an Introduction for Parents. New York: Bantam Books, 1971. Tries to help children understand what is happening to them.

Kratz, Allen W. *Stories of Significant Young Adult Ministries.* Order from The United Presbyterian Church, U.S.A., 475 Riverside Drive, Room 1164, New York, N.Y. 10115.

O'Neill, Patrick H. *The Single Adult.* New York: Paulist Press, 1979. The book speaks to the church's role in listening and speaking to the single people in its midst.

1/3 of Our Congregations, the Singles. Published in the interest of singles by the Presbyterian Church, U.S. Order from Materials Distribution Service, 341 Ponce de Leon, N.E., Atlanta, Ga. 30365. Ask for item #21680401. A guide to ministry with single persons. Includes helpful questionnaires and surveys.

Reed, Bobbie. *Developing a Single Adult Ministry.* Glendale, Calif.: International Center for Learning, 1977. A 32-page booklet for planners.

Stepfamilies: Living in Christian Harmony. St. Louis: Concordia, 1980. For all those concerned about making remarriage work.

Smoke, Jim. *Growing Through Divorce.* New York: Bantam Books, 1978. Good outline of topics to discuss with the formerly married.

Van Note, Gene, ed. *Single in a Couples' World.* Published for Aldersgate Associates by Beacon Hill Press, Kansas City, Mo.

Young Adult Living. New York: Paulist Press, 1980. For young adults and those concerned about this growing population.

Young Adult/Singles Ministry Resources. American Lutheran Church, 422 South Fifth Street, Minneapolis, Minn. 55415. A helpful mimeographed compilation of resources and ideas.

Chapter 7

Singleness and Spirituality
Holy Loneliness
By Bruce Yoder

"Don't you get lonely?" The question comes to single persons over and over again. The honest answer is, "Of course I do." Eating alone, sleeping alone, and coming home to an empty house after a hard day's work can be very lonely times. Going on vacation with no one but "me" for company or contemplating one's last years without the companionship of spouse or children team with a host of other "single" activities to sharpen the sense of isolation.

Though singleness in no way dictates that life be lived alone "ask any single person what is the greatest problem of being single and they will undoubtedly say, 'Loneliness.' "[1] Who doesn't want another person close at hand to celebrate the delights of life and share its sorrows! Who doesn't want someone to chat with about the ordinary events that form the fabric of life or to behold, in silent union, the brilliant threads of a crimson sunset! God did not design us for solitary existence, fit to wander through this world untouched.

"Don't you get lonely?" The question is a good one. The

frequency with which it is directed toward singles implies, however, that loneliness has to do with marital status. Loneliness is the problem and property of the unmarried. The question also suggests that loneliness is to be shunned. Loneliness, in reality, is a part of the human and the Christian condition. It is a fact of life and faith. Running from the experiences of loneliness is a denial of the fullness of life. Learning to live comfortably with loneliness is a sign of the mature acceptance of the richness of life.

To be lonely is to recognize that we have needs for intimate relationships that are not being met. Empty spaces exist within and between us that are not being filled. We are not being touched by God to the degree we desire. The more aware we become of these needs, the more acute is the loneliness. Yet, is it not this sense of emptiness that prompts us to open our lives to others? Is it not the ache of loneliness that pushes us to come to terms with ourselves? And, is it not our faith that only when the kingdom of God is fulfilled, we shall be personally and eternally embraced by God's love?

Loneliness keeps us moving along the path toward wholeness. It energizes the movements of growth in our life. In traditional biblical and theological terms, not until God, in an act of divine pleasure, brings "all things in heaven and on earth together," not until the glorious completion of our salvation will the question "Don't you get lonely?" be stilled (Eph. 1:10). For the honest response from both married and single persons to the matter of loneliness is, "Don't we all!" As a part of our common life, loneliness is a pain to be embraced, not pushed aside. Our deepest longings for the divine embrace of infinite love surface when we move down into this pain. So, also, the clearest perception of who we are as individual persons, creatures imaging the Creator, becomes focused in living with loneliness. Out of these two relationships—with God and with ourselves—comes a deeper and more solid appreciation for interpersonal relationships.

All human beings share a common need for human intimacy. We all want to belong, to be connected, to be known, to be touched. The pervasive temptation is to satisfy those desires prematurely, to fill the spaces of our lives quickly and overcome the threat of loneliness through our own effort. Much advertising is built upon this fundamental need for community and for a sense of well-being within oneself. In that realm, many persons recognize the seductive power and superficiality of promise, though the tugs of these marketplace remedies remain undeniably strong.

But could it be that the church is also promising more than it can deliver when loneliness is addressed? Can open, honest, loving relationships within the community of faith solve the "problem" of loneliness? The frequent questioning of singles about their feelings of loneliness and the absence of such questioning of married persons reveal a lack of appreciation in the community of faith of the necessary experience of loneliness for all. We need intimacy. Might we also need loneliness? As with viewing a dim star, it is best to look at the darkness and catch the faint glimmer out of the corner of the eye. Only by gazing into the depths of loneliness will the light of relationships be seen. This approach is lost when the church stresses only the community of believers, offering interpersonal relationships as the sole solution to loneliness.

> We indeed need each other and are able to give each other more than we often realize. Too long we have been burdened by fear and guilt, and too long we have denied each other the affection and closeness we rightly desire.

> But critical questions still need to be raised. Can real intimacy be reached without a deep respect for that holy place within us and between us...? Can human intimacy be fulfilling when every space within and between us is being filled up?[2]

Christian singles have the opportunity to be the troublesome and graceful reminders to the church and to the world that life cannot be lived well if loneliness is not accepted. A single person in the church can embody the truth that each member is a person, a unique individual. And as a separate, solitary individual each is called to respond to God. God speaks to each of us alone. To choose to respond to God, to decide to be a disciple of Jesus is to accept one's individuality. "Through the call of Jesus, men become individuals. It is no choice of their own that makes them individuals: it is Christ who makes them individuals by calling them."[3]

Surely, that call and that grace lead us into communities of belonging, mutuality, commitment, and intimacy. As Bonhoeffer notes, "The same mediator who makes us individuals is also the founder of a new fellowship. Though we all have to enter upon discipleship alone, we do not remain alone."[4] This, too, is a part of the gospel truth. That element of our faith is brought to mind by persons who are married. They are reminders, within the church, that we do not remain isolated from one another in our commitment to Christ. We are drawn into a body whose members belong to one another, whose lives intertwine in a vital way.

This truth, however, is diminished when families are esteemed as the best or only symbol of the church. Only half of the gospel is being spoken. The voice of the single person as well as the married one is needed if the whole truth is to be known. In community our aloneness, our separateness, our individuality are neither erased nor denied. Rather, they are enhanced, for it is through those qualities that we enter into relationship and through them that we continue to mature.

The situation is paradoxical. We are alone; we are together. In our aloneness we come to see that our deepest needs for unconditional love and acceptance can be met by God alone. No relationship in or out of marriage can touch the holy place within our heart that remains empty for God. No relationship, no matter how fulfilling, can take away our yearning for eternal intimacy. And no relationship can absolve us of our responsibility to respond to God's call of love. Single persons who have come to terms with this lonely dimension of life and faith witness to the truth of aloneness in the Christian life. They testify to the radically personal nature of salvation. (To say that salvation is "radically personal" is not to say that it is private.)

Married persons bring the gift of reminding us that we are together. Their vows of commitment point to the corporate nature of salvation. To be whole is to be in community; to be whole is to stand alone. The paradoxical truth of the Christian pilgrimage is spoken by two voices. Each person, whether married or single, lives the paradox. Married persons must know their aloneness just as single persons must know their connectedness. Marriage is not an excuse for not taking time to be alone. Being single is not a justification for avoiding deep commitments. Both elements are to be kept in balance within the church. At this time in the life of the church, as interpersonal relationships are rightfully receiving more attention, the single person remains a valuable witness to the *necessity* of loneliness as a part of our walk together. Having accepted and affirmed this reality, singles offer a spirituality of "holy loneliness" to the church.

As tightrope walkers, Christians can learn to trust the wire that stretches between the poles of our existence and celebrate the life made possible by the tension that exists between being alone and being in community, between our separateness and our togetherness. Our spirituality is our following after Christ on the high wire. It is a walk that must include a radically personal commitment to Jesus as Lord and a total reliance on God's grace for salvation. Peers and parents may have prepared us, but no one can walk the wire for us. Nothing brings us face-to-face with personal responsibility for ourselves as much as the decision of discipleship. Nothing allows us to see our individuality as much as God's personal address of love to each of us by name. It is the single person who is in the best position to remind the church and the world that these realities are a part of the spiritual life.

To be Christlike is our common call. An inadequate appreciation for the utter dependence upon God that marked Christ's life, an inappropriate rush to fill the empty space in all of our lives that is reserved for God, and an inability to see the process of salvation in its stark simplicity can be corrected through the spirituality of holy loneliness. To know that God is our sole companion on the way toward wholeness, to hold God as our one true lover, to keep intimate space open for God alone is to be more like Christ. This is faithful discipleship not dependent upon marriage. No one would say that such a connection should be made.

But has the church realized that "marriage, of necessity, divides one's loyalties.... The single person can concentrate with abandon on the advancement of the Kingdom of God."[5] Intensified intimacy with God can emerge as single persons affirm their singleness (whether their singleness has come through decision or default) rather than cultivate fantasies of marital intimacy. Again, this element of our Christlikeness is lost if the church assumes families are its foundation or that the loneliness of singlehood is an "unmarried" problem and not a testimony to the truth of Christian existence.

We are alone; we are together. That is one paradox of the Christian faith. A second is: we are complete; we are incomplete. While no one would suggest that marriage is a means by which to become more Christlike, many persons hold that it is a way to be more fully human. One receives from a member of the opposite sex something that is missing in one's own life, the exchange made possible simply by virtue of its taking place between a male and a female. This unbiblical notion of wholeness rests on the false assumption that, like east and west, men and women are so radically different that there is no common ground. A person can become complete only through marital union. When masculine means one set of closed qualities and feminine a separate and distinct set of other qualities, then a single person does seem to be but half a human being. Marriage is the key to wholeness.

This unscriptural myth is perpetuated when we hear women advised by Christian authors, "Femininity is acquired by accentuating the differences between yourself and men. The more different you are from men the more feminine you become. [Men are] strong, tough, firm, and heavy. [Women are] delicate, tender, gentle and light."[6]

But are we so neatly carved? Must men look outside themselves to find gentleness and women outside themselves to find strength? The Old Testament witness is that God, in whose image we are each created, is strong and tender, gentle and tough. The macho God who will "march out like a mighty man, like a warrior" is also the motherly

God who, "like a woman in childbirth, [will] cry out, gasp and pant" (Is. 42:13-14). Jesus embodied God's many emotions, purging the temple in a bold and angry confrontation with the authorities, taking onto himself the feminine symbol of wisdom, and holding on his lap children in whom he saw the key to the kingdom of God (Mt. 12:12-13; 11:19; 19:13-15). The single person who has accepted him or herself as a child of God is in a unique position to reveal the wholeness of the individual, the completeness that is grounded in God's good creation.

It is my consistent experience that each person is blessed with a blend of qualities, some of which are traditionally termed masculine, others of which are seen as feminine. To come to terms with oneself is to come to terms with one's whole self. When we affirm only a portion of who we are and decide that on the basis of culturally defined traits of the opposite sex, our self-understanding imposes limitations God never intended in the creation of the human race or in the calling to life of each of us as individuals.

As single persons come to grips with their lives, the Christian hope is that memories, dreams, emotions, thoughts, abilities, and aptitudes will all be offered to God in service and worship. Elizabeth O'Connor correctly suggests that it is the loving acceptance of "our many selves" that is part and parcel of the Christian understanding of wholeness.[7] This inclusion and integration is not possible if we believe that God made a mistake in granting us gifts that were to have been given to a member of the opposite sex. Full salvation cannot be experienced if we deny and repress who we are. Movement toward complete wholeness and harmony, or shalom, is impaired when we stake our self-acceptance on the mistaken notion that if we were made differently the path would be easier; if we were to marry we would be complete.

The rigid coupling of stereotyped feminine qualities with females and masculine traits with males fractures the biblical picture of what it means to be created as a man or a woman in the image of God. As divinely created beings, each of us is a mixture of forces that mirror God. We are each a unique swirl of dynamic energy. Carl Jung spoke of the anima and animus, the feminine and masculine forces at play within each of us. The accepting and nurturing of these different selves, integrating them into a creative, life-giving, unified self is the business of the spiritual life.

The spirituality of holy loneliness takes place in fear and trembling, for our life is in our hands. It is our responsibility and our responsibility alone to do this work of discipleship. At the same time, this spirituality is just as surely an experience of grace. God is at work within us, enabling us to move deeply into the pain of loneliness that yields greater shalom, increased wholeness, a fuller sense of life with ourselves and with God (Phil. 2:13).

The Creator has drawn us into being as complete individuals. In Christ, we see a new creation, no longer judging completeness according to predetermined categories of masculinity and femininity or of marital status (2 Cor. 5:16-17). The Spirit continues to breathe new life into creation, "con-spiring" with us to move us more fully into relationship with God. That movement is the movement of paradox. Although we are created as complete persons in the image of God, we are also incomplete. We need God and we need one another. We are intended for fellowship, both human and divine. The creation story reveals that clearly. The fellowship, however, is not a compensation for our incompleteness as individual men and women. To move in that direction is to say that God's creation was severely faulted, that a person was not a real person imaging his or her creator.

No. We are complete; we are incomplete. It is a paradox. The self-acceptance that affirms completeness in oneself is also that acceptance of loneliness that reminds us of our incompleteness. This self-acceptance is a crucial step in the movement of one's Christian life, a step made possible when we face our aloneness.

The spirituality of holy loneliness, or of solitude, is possible when we no longer see loneliness as an experience from which to flee but one, rather, that we willingly enter. By entering the pain and darkness of being alone, fearful emptiness becomes holy loneliness. Loneliness is transformed from being a frightening experience, a wrestling with the dark angels of our soul, to a time of quietness and blessing. It is this movement that some have termed the movement "from loneliness to solitude."[8] It is the change from feeling ill at ease with aloneness to being at home with it.

Relationships are examined best if we look away from them first. We try to look directly at the dim star and it fades into oblivion. By recognizing beforehand that there are needs God alone can meet—absolute understanding, complete acceptance, unconditional love—and by seeing first of all the goodness of ourselves as individuals gifted by God we have looked into dark loneliness and discovered that it is a valued part of life. From such a spirituality of solitude will spring healthy, nourishing relationships.

One way of noting the maturity with which the two paradoxes of the spiritual life (alone: together; complete: incomplete) are embodied is to note our expectations of others. Henri Nouwen has observed that "the basic human condition of aloneness has entered so deeply into emotional awareness that we are constantly tempted to want more of our fellow human beings than they can give."[9]

Now let us look directly at those relationships. When we

believe someone can take away our private pain, loneliness has become a trap. It will be a bottomless pit. Failing to come to terms with the above may generate a flurry of activities as we search for the one person, one church, one job, one city that holds the key to our happiness. A life crammed full of worthwhile endeavors and stimulating people may signify a passive resignation to the task of owning one's loneliness. A whirlwind may indicate the futile search of a tired soul. St. Augustine put it well: "Lord, we are restless until we find our rest in thee."

Holy loneliness is marked by stillness. Quietness that does not scramble for attention and affection characterizes the life of one who knows loneliness is part of life. Such solitude is found only when the pain of loneliness has been embraced, when life is not packed with activities like a suitcase before a two-week vacation. The gift of the single person to the church is to "protect that emptiness for God," an emptiness present in all persons and in all relationships.[10] Singles who embody a spirituality of solitude are the gentle, individual reminders that our movement toward shalom, toward wholeness and harmony with our Creator and the created world, neither denies nor removes our aloneness. As we have noted, coming to terms with one's loneliness opens the door for a deep relationship of intimacy with God, a relationship that touches the seemingly unreachable recesses of our lives. It also opens us to others.

We are alone; we are together. We are complete; we are incomplete. The balance of tension within each of these paradoxes produces solid relationships of care, also marked by a paradox: attachment, detachment. As we relax our desperate hold on others, a hold strengthened by the myths that others will make us complete and that loneliness is a problem to be eradicated through relationships, we actually begin to embrace the other person as a person.

Solitude is being at home with oneself; intimacy is being at home with another. Rarely can one happen without the other. "Let him who cannot be alone beware of community." "Let him who is not in community beware of being alone."[11] Loving relationships of integrity emerge and are strengthened when the two sides of life are kept in creative tension. Dark and frightening loneliness that has become the holy loneliness of solitude paves the way for friendships of care and devotion.

Members of Protestant religious communities have remarked that the caring development of relationships which emerge between celibate individuals during times of prayer, service, and sharing is excellent preparation for marriage.[12] Not expecting others to save us from ourselves, not fostering the dreams and illusions we project onto others, we realize the power of loneliness is transformed from a destructive and divisive force to one that brings us together. "In deep solitude . . . I find the gentleness with which I can truly love my brothers."[13]

The gift of God's presence is most often granted in relationships with other persons. Through their love, we come to know love. Through their forgiveness, we experience forgiveness. There is no denying the reality of incarnate grace. Singleness is an opportunity to develop relationships of deep love and affection with both men and women. There God is found.

To experience that grace most fully, single and married persons alike do well to remember that, within the relationship, it is God who is embracing us. It is God alone who meets us in the depths of our soul. The spirituality of solitude affirms this underlying truth as it moves deeply into the pain of loneliness. Through the love and care of others divine grace becomes real. The reality of that love may well be necessary for an individual to strike out alone into the dark night. But there comes a time when all who seek wholeness must enter that void. Within the spirituality of solitude, we do not forget that emptiness will always be present, even in the fullest of friendships. From that loneliness we will not shy away for holy loneliness reminds us that just as God dwells in the fullness of human love, so also God dwells in our emptiness.

Notes

1. Letha Scanzoni and Nancy Hardesty, *All We're Meant to Be* (Waco, Tex.: Word Books, 1974), p. 163.

2. Henri Nouwen, *Clowning in Rome* (Garden City, N.Y.: Image Books, 1979), pp. 39-40.

3. Dietrich Bonhoeffer, *The Cost of Discipleship* (New York: Macmillan, 1967), p. 113.

4. *Ibid.*, p. 112.

5. Richard Foster, *Freedom of Simplicity* (New York: Harper and Row, 1981), p. 136.

6. Marilyn McGinnis, *Single* (Old Tappan, N.J.: Pillar Books, 1976), pp. 69-70.

7. Elizabeth O'Connor, *Our Many Selves* (New York: Harper and Row, 1971), Part 1.

8. Henri Nouwen, *Reaching Out* (Garden City, N.Y.: Doubleday, 1975), see Part 1.

9. *Op. cit., Clowning in Rome*, pp. 40-41

10. *Ibid.*, p. 45.

11. Dietrich Bonhoeffer, *Life Together* (New York: Harper and Row, 1954), pp. 77-78.

12. Charles Fracchia, *Living Together Alone* (New York: Harper and Row, 1979), p. 20.

13. Thomas Merton, *The Sign of Jonas* (Garden City, N.Y.: Image Books, 1956), p. 261.

Reflection and Discussion Guide

Reflection and Discussion Guide

The material for this book has been drawn primarily from the lives of men and women who are now single or who have been so most of their adult life. Their thoughts and experiences have been offered as mirror in which others may take a new look at issues of singleness, such as sexuality, spirituality, and professionalism, within the context of the church. Personal reflection is a most beneficial tool in addressing life's issues. That is true for both author and reader.

As is noted in many of the chapters, the closer we move to the heart of a concern the more we see that married and single persons alike have to deal with very similar experiences as they relate to friends, jobs, themselves, and God. The line between married and single persons is often too sharply drawn.

So, too, is the line between author and reader. It is our hope that this line will be erased as you who use this book move from hearing about the experiences of others to examining your own life. To that end this guide for reflection and discussion is presented.

Many of the questions and suggestions that are offered below are addressed to single persons who are reading this book alone. Others are directed toward groups of single persons who are using it as a basis for discussion. Still others are addressed to individuals who are married. A quick glance at the questions will reveal that almost all of them could be used in any of the above settings. The readers are urged to adapt them to their own particular use.

Each chapter has fifteen to twenty questions that are arranged to follow the development of the material as it is presented in the body of the book. For maximum benefit to be gained from the guide, do *not* attempt to respond to all of the questions. Deal with those that strike you as being important for you and let the rest go by. If the book is being used in a group setting, a leader may choose to focus on only one or two questions. A handful of active participants will easily fill an evening's discussion as they deal with the issues that are raised.

For persons who are reading this book alone, we offer the following suggestions. After you have selected the questions to which you want to respond, write your answers in a notebook. Skimming over the guide will not get you to move deeply into your own life. Taking time to write down your thoughts will help you to move in that direction. The notebook is yours, so don't worry about spelling, grammar, or handwriting. The important point is for you to express your honest feelings as they are brought to the surface by the questions that touch you. Having done this, you may wish to share your answers with a trusted friend.

The questions in the guide are purposefully flexible. When it is suggested that you chart experiences, for example, no set time period is offered. You may be in a position to examine the experiences of singleness over a ten-year period while someone else will scan forty years. Always take the question into your setting and make it fit your needs so that you can move freely into your thoughts and feelings.

It is our hope that what has been shared by these seven brothers and sisters is but the opening statement in a long and fruitful conversation.

—The editors.

Chapter 1

Singleness and Relationships
From Rebellion to Celebration

1. Developmental stages are not neat, well-marked categories through which we pass never to return to them again. Rather, the stages are identifiable experiences that relate to one another according to one's own personality and development. A person may pass through rebellion at one level in his or her life and then return to it at a deeper level years later. Or rebellion may characterize part of one's reaction to singleness while affirmation marks another part of that person's response to singleness at the same time. What stages of development are you able to see in your life? Which is the most prominent?

2. Draw a lifeline of your singlehood, plotting the most significant stage for each time period of your adult life.

Write down the experience that most symbolizes the stage you were at in each time period of your life. For example: 18—rebellion—did not have a close friend of the opposite sex.

3. Discuss the statement "trying to find our happiness and fulfillment in another person destroys nourishing relationships because it makes impossible demands on them." Are there examples in your life in which the pressure to make someone happy has been put on you? How did that pressure affect the relationship?

4. Do you think that marriage will make an unhappy person happy? Why or why not?

5. What do you think the author means when she says that sin is separation and isolation?

6. If total dependence is 1 on a scale from 1 to 10 and total independence is 10, where would you rank yourself? Are you happy where you are? What would it take to move in the direction you desire?

7. The writer says, "Alienation from self causes unhappiness and loneliness." Explore the areas of your life in which you are unhappy or lonely. Are you out of touch with yourself in those areas?

8. The writer suggests that some people blame their parents, spouses, bosses, and close friends for their unhappiness without ever assuming responsibility for their own happiness. How true is this of you?

9. What is your experience of rating or being rated as "mate material"? Compare the responses of men and women if you are studying this chapter with a group of friends. Another form of this pressure is that of third-party "well-wishers" who push persons who are dating to "get moving down the aisle." Have you experienced this pressure and how did it affect your relationship?

10. When a person celebrates his or her singleness, others often perceive that individual as closing the door to marital possibilities. However, it is precisely the person who is joyfully content in life who is the freest to offer love and make healthy commitments. Why do you believe the discrepancy between these two positions exists?

11. It is usually maintained that depression is anger turned inward. Dorothy Gish notes that this stage of depression may be the "mad at God" stage. Could it be, however, that fear of owning and expressing anger toward God locks persons in this stage? That is to say, as a person becomes angry with God, they have the key to move out of this stage. Do you see depression and anger linked in your life? Is it okay for persons to be mad at God?

12. Find examples of the "fulfillment myth" as it is spread by the mass media. In advertisement, whether the product is soap or a car, what is being communicated about the need for a person of the opposite sex?

13. In your church experience, are persons who are not married viewed as those who didn't "make it"? How is this judgment communicated?

14. In what ways can you identify with the statement "Marriage? who needs it!"

15. The author noted that the motivating force behind some of her accomplishments was powered, in part, by repressed desires. Repression can be a source of energy, though it is not the healthiest form. What are the ways you can tell in your life whether your desires to succeed, to accomplish a goal or fulfill obligations, are coming from repressions or from self-acceptance?

16. God is the source of our self-acceptance. Because God loves us we can love ourselves. The church has been called to communicate this divine acceptance. How is your church enabling you to love and accept yourself? In what ways are you assisting others in this process?

17. For this exercise, file folder labels and pens are needed for each member of the group. Sit in a circle and select one member of the group to be "bombarded with love." In silence, each of the other members of the group writes at least one positive thing about that other member on a label. After a minute of writing, everyone sticks their label on the person, saying aloud what they have written. Move around the group bombarding each person separately. Take some time at the end of the exercise to discuss your feelings.

18. Do you perceive your singleness as a gift? Why or why not? Do you see it as a choice?

19. List the privileges and opportunities that singleness offers you.

20. Affirmation of oneself and emotional well-being are essential to have close friends of both sexes. List your closest friends. Note if they are men or women. Note also if they are older, younger, or the same age as you. Are they single or married? How do you feel about the scope of your friendship?

21. The church often celebrates motherhood on Mother's Day, fatherhood on Father's Day. Weddings celebrate the beginning of a marriage; baby dedications, the new life given to a couple. Design a service to celebrate singleness and suggest to your pastor that this service be held some Sunday morning.

Chapter 2

Singles and Professionalism
Rejection Slips and Spaghetti Suppers

1. A profession is "any job in which one has to make informed decisions." If there are persons within your study group who fit this description, ask them to discuss the relationship that they see between being single and having a profession. Do they agree with the author that career affects a marriage decision minimally while the choice to remain single opens more doors to a professional career?

2. Ask a group of young adults who are on the threshold of their careers how much risk-taking they believe they can afford. In this group include single persons, married persons without children, and married persons with children. Do the answers you receive fit with the author's observations?

3. Do singles in your fellowship provide the "spirit of freedom" the author suggests is theirs to give? Is this a welcomed contribution or does it get in the way of "family stability"? What are the assets and liabilities of freedom within the life of the church? What are the assets and liabilities of discipline?

4. Do you agree with the author's assessment that the church has become too domestic and family-oriented? Cite examples from the life of your congregation.

5. A healthy marriage provides a context in which to process the ups and downs of professional life. In what job-related situa-

tions do you most experience the absence of that "already-there relationship" in which you can process those difficulties? Do you take responsibility to find persons when you need to work through these job-related issues?

6. In her chapter on "Friendship," Dorothy Gish spoke of repression as a motivating force for overachievers. This author points to the same force as he indicates the temptation to substitute success for personal affection. Are there areas in your life in which you have made this substitution?

7. Singles find it easier to take risks in a career than married people. Yet, the author states that we hesitate to develop relationships of intimacy and genuine care for the same reason—risks. How do you experience these two types of risk-taking? Is it true that the predictability of rewards in professional life tends to keep us from investing in personal relationships?

8. List the persons in your primary support group. How many of these individuals are "professional friends" and how many would remain your friend if you switched professions? Who are the persons who help you love yourself? How do they do this?

9. Are single persons more in danger of becoming enamored with the money they make than married persons? In most marriages, spouses discuss family money matters. Is there a similar process for single persons? Money is also a source of contention in many marriages. Are single persons better off because they manage their money on their own? Or is this a dangerous position to be in?

10. In practical ways, what does it mean for you to love yourself? Where is the line between moderation and excessive care of yourself? On the other hand, how do you draw the line between giving to others and being taken advantage of by them?

11. Some single persons in the church say they are often ignored or not used in church life. Others, however, tell of being pressed into service because they could not offer the "excuse" of having to give time to their family. Where do you fit into this picture? What would it take for you to say, "I want to be used more" or "No, I need time for myself"?

12. How do you relieve the tension of your profession? What do you do to play?

13. Draw a circle representing the sum total of your waking

hours. Cut the pie into wedges according to the amount of time you give to your job, your friends, your church, yourself. Are you satisfied with the proportions? Where and how would you like to make changes, if any?

14. "Who are you?" Write ten sentences or phrases as quickly as they come to mind. How many of these are related to your professional life?

15. "In the most important parts of life I am really not all that different from other people." Yet, in the next paragraph the author urges singles to "search for our unique humanity" with reckless abandon. First describe the meaningful areas of your life that you hold in common with others. Then list the ways that you see yourself as a unique individual.

16. Respond to the description of Jesus as one who "was intoxicated with the richness and goodness of life."

Chapter 3

Single in a Married Society
Where Is My Family?

1. The author began her chapter with an illustration from her childhood which illustrates how children's games can reinforce stereotypes of singles. Think of your childhood and try to recall what games or sayings promoted stereotypes regarding singles.

2. Often we receive unspoken (implied) or spoken messages that tell us what we should do. Think about any messages you received as to whether or not you should marry and have children, then attempt to discover who sent you these messages. In order to help you identify who sent you these messages, write the socialization agents on one side and the messages received on the other side of a piece of paper or on the chalkboard (if doing this exercise in a group).

Socialization Agent	Messages Received
Family	
School	
Church	
Peers	
Relatives	
Larger Community	
Other	

3. The author states that we are prepared for the adult role of

marriage and parenthood from early childhood, rather than being prepared for the option of singleness. Think about your childhood. In terms of the toys, were you given dolls, a variety of toys, only trucks?

4. If your parents are still living, talk to them about what they were taught regarding singleness, marriage, and parenthood. Ask them about their socialization in this regard.

5. If you cannot interview your parents, think about and complete this sentence:

My mother would say _____ in regard to singleness.

My father would say _____ in regard to singleness.

6. If you are doing these exercises in a group, divide into pairs and share stories which illustrate how your sex role socialization affects your current behavior. Following that, share in the larger group.

7. The author raises two questions: What are the possibilities for role models in your social structure, and what in your culture might have influenced you to choose one model over another? (Again, you might need to share stories to facilitate recall.)

8. The author indicates that the age of 20-28 is the time of forming your adult identity, i.e., integrating your own values system and establishing a lifestyle upon which initial choices are made. Several years ago one group of singles made the following statement: "The greatest pressure to marry and least acceptance of singleness comes not from the family, nor from other religious groups, nor from secular society, but from the ... church." Does that statement model your situation? If not, from whom do you experience the greatest pressure to marry?

9. At the same retreat referred to in the above question, all singles under 35 thought of themselves as temporarily single. When do you consider persons to be more than temporarily single? If you are single, do you view your single state as temporary?

10. One of the first ways to resocialize yourself, is to reject the idea that you are inferior and begin to feel good about yourself. The author indicates that society was more helpful in affirming her singleness than the church. What has been your experience in that regard?

11. What were you taught about singleness, according to the Bible? Are these passages in the Old Testament or the New Testament? If verses from the Old Testament come to mind, ask yourself if you were taught to literally interpret these Scriptures. Furthermore, how do you explain this if you believe that the Old Testament was preparatory in nature, and the New Testament was the final revelation.

12. What relationship do you see between economics and our own attitudes and practices toward marriage?

13. The author suggests that our culture and traditions have kept us from following the example of Christ, who broke with the structures of his culture. Do you agree or disagree with this? Give examples. (This would be a good time to share experiences.)

14. Talk about the myths that you have been taught regarding marriage and singleness. How have these myths created barriers between married and single persons. (If this is a group exercise, you might divide up into twos and attempt to put one single and one married person in each pair.)

15. The author indicates that the church gives singles mixed messages on sexual expression. On one side of a paper or chalkboard list the concerns that you have had in regard to sexual expression and any other topic relating to singleness, and on the other side write how the church has responded to that concern. If you are married, do the same thing in regard to your concerns.

Concerns   **Church's Response**

16. Divide the group into pairs (single and married). Have the singles talk to married persons for five minutes about their concerns regarding singleness. Married persons can only express affirmative comments, expressing understanding, and encourage the singles to continue expressing their feelings. Then reverse roles and have the single persons listen to the married persons, and repeat the exercise. This could work well with singles and their parents as well.

17. The author, in discussing the church, states we are not, in fact, powerless if we follow the New Testament model of the church. Her idea is that the church could form a task force to

examine curriculum which would not leave out or stereotype singles. Find some Sunday school material and examine it to see if the curriculum does leave out singles. Report to the group if you are studying this in the context of a group. Decide if your church does, in fact, need a task force.

18. One of the values of the General Conference deaconess program was the supportive network it provided for single women. Since singles need a supportive network in the departure from the traditional family structure, think of ways singles' needs could be met.

19. The author raises various questions about other possibilities that might be helpful (see page 47). You will note that one possibility suggested is that of a kind of dispersed "order." John Howard Yoder, a Mennonite theologian, in his unpublished paper "Singleness in Ethical and Pastoral Perspective," describes such an order in the following way: a group of singles who morally support one another, with periodic retreats, a circle letter, with shared disciplines and shared work of particular problems. Discuss this idea and the other possibilities mentioned.

20. Look up Acts 2:42-47. What do you think about developing small households of God in an effort to work at Koinonia?

Chapter 4

Singleness and Scripture
Bible Stories for Singles

1. What is your response to the suggestion that single persons fit into the biblical category of "widows and orphans," persons for whom the church is supposed to offer special care?

2. The author sets herself off from two groups she saw in the congregation, the "mainstreamers" who were okay and those who had special needs requiring attention. What is your experience in finding a niche in your congregation? Why did she resist the formation of a group for singles? How does her thinking fit or not fit your situation?

3. Wounds are produced by internal contradictions of which we are unaware. How does becoming aware of the tension reduce the hurt? Or doesn't it?

4. References to singleness *per se* in Scripture are rare. Read Matthew 19:12 and 1 Corinthians 7. In what ways do these passages speak to you?

5. Rather than look directly at the references above, the author has chosen to examine the scriptural picture of wholeness. Why has she done this? What can be learned about singleness in Scripture by surveying biblical pictures of wholeness?

6. "Most of us exist because somebody else wanted us to." Do you have that belief about yourself? In Richmond, Virginia, over half of the babies born in 1979 were born out of wedlock. This is

110 / Single Voices

not to say these children were not wanted. Children born within a traditional, nuclear family may not be wanted. Yet that statistic, as well as others, raises hard questions. Is the life of each infant "God's idea in the first place"? How can an unwanted child become wanted?

7. The creation story affirms that our lives are a gift of grace, that each person is a whole person, and that everyone has a vocation. Do you see these affirmations in the creation account and in your life? Where?

8. Identify places in your life where you, like Sarah, have given up an impossible dream. What was it you wanted? Has it come to you in unexpected ways or has the dream vanished unfulfilled?

9. Wholeness, says the author, is rooted in parental and divine love and hope. How does this mesh with your experience? If you are unsure of your parents' love and hope, can you be whole?

10. Spend half an hour daily at least four times during one week meditating on Psalm 139:13-15. Write down your thoughts and feelings. Record images that come to mind. Share the experience with others who have also done the meditation.

11. The parallel between the dream of Sarah and the dream of a single person is not between that of wanting a child and wanting a spouse. The author's point is that creative single living is possible when identity and self-image are connected to God's dynamic and unpredictable movement. Where have you felt God nudging you in a certain direction but have held back because it seemed ridiculous to move that way? Is there a constant ending to "Someday I'm going to _____." Could that be the Spirit in you wanting to give birth to new life? Share some of these nudgings with others and see where they might lead.

12. Discuss the creation of woman as depicted in this chapter. Are you seeing any elements of it for the first time?

13. In what ways does loneliness emerge from a life of abundance?

14. Do you agree that vocation includes obstacles? To what vocation have you been called and what blocks are there that hinder you from carrying out your calling? What sort of "fruitfulness" is evident within your vocation?

15. The "creative task" of Jesus moved him beyond loyalty to

his family clan. While singleness is often perceived to enhance the movement beyond family, it is also true that many single persons are expected to care for ailing parents because other brothers and sisters "have their own families." Have you experienced this tension? In what ways has your singleness freed you to move beyond "biological loyalties"? How has it hindered such movement?

16. Discuss the Jephthah story. What would you do if you were in the role of the daughter? If your death were imminent, what particular loss would you "bewail"?

17. What do you believe is the highest contribution persons can make to their community? Where would you rate marriage and procreation? List all of the offerings you make to your church community or to a close circle of friends. Arrange them in order of importance. Ask a friend to list the contributions you make and prioritize them. Compare the lists and share.

18. Where in your life are there unrealized possibilities? Where is life unlived? As these areas are identified share with others in order to discern if these unfulfilled dreams are like those of Sarah or if they are parts of life to mourn and let go. The author notes that mourning and affirming life are closely related. Compare the Sarah and Jephthah's daughter stories, as well as your own experiences to discover this relationship.

Chapter 5

Singles and Sexuality
A Gift from God

1. What does it mean for you to be a sexual being? What words, feelings, and experiences come to mind as you think about yourself as a sexual person?
2. Do you experience your sexuality as a gift?
3. Through the story of creation we see that all persons are sexual beings, intended for relationship. However, it often occurs that only married persons are perceived as sexual beings. Recount experiences in which you as a single person have felt treated as a non-sexual person.
4. How does your picture of God change when you see that the divine image contains both male and female forces?
5. Discuss the prime male and female encounters you have had which reflect God's being. Do you believe you can reflect who God is without a significant relationship with a member of the opposite sex? Why or why not?
6. Respond to the definitions of sex and sexuality. Does the distinction between the two made by the author make sense to you?
7. What does it mean to you to be a "body-self"? That is, what does it mean for you to *be* a body, not just have a body?
8. The author states that married persons have greater freedom to experience their genital sexuality than do single adults.

Reflection and Discussion Guide / 113

But, when singles are in touch with their affective sexuality they may be more sexually mature than married persons. Do you believe this is true? Also, if a single adult is sexually mature do you believe he or she should have the freedom to experience more fully his or her genital sexuality? Is sexual intercourse between single adults ever appropriate? Why or why not? What are appropriate biblical texts to consider? Do you think that sexual guidelines for responsible single adults should be the same as for teenagers?

9. Discuss guidelines for sexual behavior among single and married adults.

10. One common mistake the author points to in our understanding of sexuality is the overemphasis on genital sexuality. If genital sexual activity in a relationship precedes the emotional, intellectual, spiritual interchange, the latter may be blocked. Discuss the practical implications of a "nonintegrated" relationship in which genital sexual activity is the primary focus.

11. If our genital sexual feelings are seen as bad and are repressed, the repression may intensify our desires and block our experience of affective sexual feelings. What are ways you believe singles can accept and affirm their physical sexual desires?

12. Place yourself on a continuum between mind and body. Are you primarily oriented toward thinking or feeling, toward knowledge or emotions?

13. Share some stories from your adolescent life that describe ways you experienced your sexuality. What role did peers in school play? Friends from church? Parents?

14. Has sexuality ever been discussed in your congregation? What type of program, class, or group would you find most helpful in addressing your questions about sexuality? What can you do to see that these issues are picked up by your church?

15. The author states that, since "we are sexual beings created in the image of God, the spiritual, emotional, and psychological aspects of intimacy must take precedence over the physical." To what extent do you agree or disagree?

16. "Friendship does not imply the need for genital interaction." However, persons in touch with their genital and affective sexuality may well have sexual feelings of attraction in a deep friendship. If this has been true for you, how were these feelings handled? Do you talk about sexual feelings with close friends of

114 / Single Voices

the opposite sex? Does it make a difference if this person is married or single?

17. One way members of a congregation can give physical expression to their love for one another is through touch. An affectionate hug or embrace can communicate Christian care. Does this happen within your fellowship? How do you feel about the level of affection in your congregation? Do single persons have more freedom to express this side of love than do married persons?

18. How does your picture of Jesus change if you think about him as a sexual person with both genital and affective sexual drives and desires? How does this affect your relationship with him?

19. Jesus is a model of gentleness, tenderness, compassion. (We also know that anyone who carpentered, walked the long roads of Palestine, and confronted authorities was strong, tough, and assertive.) How do the men in your group see the first three qualities listed being expressed in their lives?

20. What relationship do you now have that best embodies God's love? In what ways does this relationship also affirm your sexuality?

Chapter 6

Singleness and the Church
Models for Singles Ministries

1. How would you explain the New Testament concept of the church such that single persons are included and not second-rate members when compared to families?

2. How many single persons are members of your congregation? Talk to the single persons in your church. Do you discover as the author suggests that age difference is accompanied by differing needs? What are those needs and in what ways can your congregation better respond to them?

3. For singles: list all of the words that come to mind when you say the word "single." Ask a group of married persons to make a similar response. Compare the two lists.

4. Many single persons maintain that the church is the hardest place to find acceptance as a person. Has this been the experience of singles in your group? What blocks have been put in the way? How do you think they can be removed? What role can you play in the church's acceptance of you as a single adult?

5. Is your pastor supportive of single persons in the congregation? How is that support shown or withheld? Perhaps you might want to arrange a meeting in which your concerns are shared with your pastor.

6. Passivity on the part of singles may well mean an absence of church programming directed toward their interests. What would

it mean for you to take responsibility for applying "appropriate pressure on the church ministry" or being your own advocate in order for the church to minister better to all of its members?

7. How would your church respond to the question "Do you have a class for skeptics?" Is there room for asking faith questions?

8. Is there interest in your congregation among both married and single persons to discuss issues related to singleness? Meet with these persons some evening to decide if you want to form a small group, a new Sunday school class, or have a Sunday evening series with the larger congregation.

9. What books are in your library pertaining to single issues? Make a list of books that would be helpful or of needs you want books to address. Meet with the librarian to see if some of these books can be added to your church library.

10. Are there divorced persons in your congregation? How are they accepted? Have divorced persons chosen not to attend because they feel they would be rejected? How might a "divorce recovery event" such as the one the author described be helpful? Contact persons who have attended events such as a retreat for the formerly married held yearly at Laurelville Mennonite Church Center. Have them talk about their experience.

11. As nuclear families in our society face increasing pressure, the church will be called upon to provide increasing support for them. This comes at a time when ministry to singles is also receiving more attention. How can possible tension between ministry to families and ministry to singles be lessened in your church?

12. What are the words that come to mind when you say the word "divorce." Compare lists written by individuals who are divorced and by some who are not. What do the lists indicate about the level of understanding or communication between the two groups?

13. What is your congregation's response to remarriage following a divorce? Has it considered the biblical teachings and the needs of these persons?

14. What church-sponsored programs are available for singles in your area? If there is an absence of ministry for single persons, what one program might your church initiate?

15. In what ways are death and divorce similar? In what ways are they different? How have you seen persons in your congrega-

Reflection and Discussion Guide / 117

tion respond to a member who has lost a spouse through death? through divorce?

16. Have any persons in your congregation volunteered a year or two of their lives in Christian service? Does your congregation encourage its young adults to enter these church programs? Single persons may well have more time and energy for these commitments. This is a valuable gift to the church that singles have to offer.

17. Check the do's and don'ts at the end of the article. What is your reaction to the author's list? Where are you in agreement? How does your church program rate?

Chapter 7

Singles and Spirituality
Holy Loneliness

1. What are the times in which you experienced the greatest feelings of loneliness? The author states that these experiences are an inevitable part of the Christian life. Do you agree?

2. Is it your experience as a single person that the question "Don't you get lonely?" is addressed more often to you than to married persons?

3. "Loneliness keeps us moving along the path toward wholeness?" Is this true for you, and if so, how?

4. The Christian life contains elements of aloneness and individuality as well as elements of community and connectedness. With a group of persons through conversation with one another, place yourself physically on an "aloneness continuum" that has "at home with being alone" at one end of the room and "ill at ease with being alone" at the other. Repeat the exercise on a "community continuum." Finally, try to place yourself through conversation with others on the "Christian continuum" with aloneness at one end and community at the other. What do you discover in the third step of this exercise? Discuss your feelings after each step.

5. What is your reaction to the statement that "the gift of singles to the church is the spirituality of solitude, holy loneliness"? The author states that single persons who have accepted their

"holy loneliness" witness to the radically personal nature of salvation. Persons who have freely chosen marriage witness to the corporate nature of salvation. How well does your congregation hear both of these voices?

6. Discuss the Bonhoeffer quote: "Through the call of Jesus men [and women] become individuals."

7. It is well known that intimate relationships require work. No marriage remains strong and healthy if both husband and wife do not take time for the relationship. What are ways that you cultivate your relationship of intimacy with God?

8. List qualities traditionally termed masculine or feminine. Which qualities do you have? Are some of these qualities drawn from the "opposite sex" side? Do you perceive those characteristics as being assets or liabilities?

9. How different do you believe men and women are in their emotional and spiritual makeup?

10. Explore passages in the Bible that speak of God in feminine terms: Ps. 132; Is. 49:15; 66:9; Lk. 15:8-10.

11. What part of yourself do you have the most trouble accepting? Is this tied to the traditional definition of what it means to be a man or a woman?

12. One description of discipleship is movement toward wholeness where wholeness is understood to be the divine peace, or shalom, that puts all of creation into harmony with itself and its Creator. Chart on a graph your movement toward wholeness, describing both high and low points on this journey.

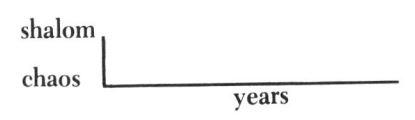

```
shalom |
 chaos |_____
          years
```

13. Think about the last time that you were alone with yourself. Were you at home with yourself or did you feel ill at ease? Were you settled or distracted? What were the things you thought about during that time?

14. We expect friends, especially Christian friends, to share life with us, both its joys and its sorrows. The author suggests that it is unreasonable to expect someone to relieve us of our pain or to attend to our needs all the time. Discuss the limitations of each posi-

tion, and the ways in which they complement each other.

15. List all of the things you do during the course of a normal week that are not job-related. Do any of these activities appear to be an effort to avoid being alone with yourself?

16. In what ways does coming to terms with your own loneliness open you to others? Give specific examples of relationships that have blossomed because you are more deeply rooted in yourself.

Bibliography

The following list of resources, while extensive, is not comprehensive. Titles included reflect a diversity of views, and the editors of this book do not endorse the entire contents of all publications listed.

Books
Adams, Margaret. *Single Blessedness*. New York: Basic Books, 1976.
Andrews, Gini. *Sons of Freedom, God & the Single Man*. Grand Rapids, Mich.: Zondervan, 1975.
──────── *Your Half of the Apple, God and the Single Girl*. Grand Rapids, Mich.: Zondervan, 1972.
Barkas, J. L. *Single in America*. New York: Athaneum, 1980. Zondervan, 1972.
Beachy, Bertha. "Single Mennonite Women Serving Abroad" in *Which Way Women?* ed. Dorothy Yoder Nyce, Akron, Pa.: Mennonite Central Committee Peace Section, 1980.
Board, C. Stephen, et al. *Guide to Sex, Singleness & Marriage*. Downers Grove, Ill.: InterVarsity, 1974.
Bequaret, Lucia H. *Single Women Alone and Together*. Boston: Beacon Press, 1976.
Bontrager, Frances M. *The Church and the Single Person*. Scottdale: Herald Press, 1969.
Bontrager, G. Edwin. *Divorce and the Faithful Church*. Scottdale: Herald Press, 1978.

Brown, Raymond Kay. *Reach Out to Singles: A Challenge to Ministry.* Philadelphia: Westminster Press, 1979.

Brown, Velma Darbo. *After Weeping.* Nashville: Broadman Press, 1980.

Christoff, Nicholas B. *Saturday Night, Sunday Morning: Singles and the Church.* New York: Harper & Row, 1978.

Clarkson, Margaret. *So You're Single.* Wheaton, Ill.: Harold Shaw, 1978.

Collins, Gary R. *It's O.K. to Be Single.* Waco, Tex.: Word Books, 1976.

Craig, Floyd A. *How to Communicate with Single Adults.* Nashville: Broadman Press, 1978.

Drescher, John M. and Sandra Drescher. *When You Think You're in Love.* St. Meinrad, Ind.: Abbey Press, 1981, see pp. 84-90.

Edwards, Marie and Eleanor. *The Challenge of Being Single.* Los Angeles: J. P. Tarcher, Inc., 1974.

Evening, Margaret. *Who Walk Alone: A Consideration of the Single Life.* Downers Grove, Ill.: InterVarsity, 1974.

Fix, Janet and Lola Levitt. *For Singles Only.* Old Tappan, N.J.: Revell, 1978.

Fracchia, Charles. *Living Together Alone.* New York: Harper and Row, 1979.

Funk, Herta. "The Single Life" in *Which Way Women?* ed. Dorothy Yoder Nyce, Akron, Pa.: Mennonite Central Committee Peace Section, 1980.

Gardner, Richard A., MD. *The Boys and Girls Book about Divorce.* New York: Bantam, 1971.

────── *The Boys and Girls Book About One-Parent Families.* New York: Putnam, 1978.

Gilder, George. *Naked Nomads, Unmarried Men in America.* New York: The New York Times Book Company, 1974.

Goergen, Donald. *The Sexual Celibate.* New York: Seabury Press, 1974.

Hart, Patrick. *Thomas Merton: The Monastic Journey.* Kansas City: Andrews and McMeel, Inc., 1977.

Hiesberger, Jean M., ed. *Young Adult Living Handbook.* New York: Paulist Press, 1980.

Jackson, Dave and Neta. *Living Together in a World Falling Apart.* Carol Stream, Ill.: Creation House, 1974.

Jepson, Sarah. *For the Love of Singles.* Carol Stream, Ill.: Creation House, 1970.

Kaymeyer, C. W. 2nd ed. *Confronting the Issues: Marriage and the Family, and Sex Roles.* Boston: Allyn and Bacon, Inc., 1981. See section one, "The Basic Issue: To Marry or Remain Single," pp. 9-57.

Krantzler, Mel. *Creative Divorce.* New York: M. Evans & Co., Inc., 1974.

Lum, Ada. *Single and Human.* Downers Grove, Ill.: InterVarsity Press, 1976.

Lyon, William. *A Pew for One, Please: The Church and the Single Person*. New York: Seabury Press, 1977.
Martin, John R. *Divorce and Remarriage*. Scottdale: Herald Press, 1974.
Martin, Norma and Zola Levitt. *Divorce: A Christian Dilemma*. Scottdale: Herald Press, 1977.
McAllaster, Elva. *Free to Be Single*. Chappaqua, N.Y.: Christian Herald Books, 1979.
McGinnis, Marilyn. *Single*. Old Tappan, N.J.: Revell, 1974.
Melville, Keith, ed. *Marriage and Family*. New York: Random House, 1977. See chapter five, "Choosing the Single Life—In the Land of the Married," pp. 119-148.
Merton, Thomas. *The Sign of Jonas*. Garden City, N.Y.: Image Books, 1956.
Miller, Keith and Andrea Miller. *Christian Living—Personal Faith—Growth*. Waco: Word Books, 1981.
Miller, John W. *A Christian Approach to Sexuality*. Scottdale: Mennonite Publishing House, 1973. See chapter twelve, "Sexual Healing for the Unmarried," pp. 93-104.
Murdock, Carol Vejvoda. *Single Parents Are People Too: How to Achieve a Positive Self-Image and Personal Satisfaction*. New York: Butterick Pub., 1980.
Mumaw, Evelyn King. *Woman Alone*. Scottdale: Herald Press, 1970.
Nelson, James B. *Embodiment: An Approach to Sexuality and Christian Theology*. See chapter seven, "The Morality of Sexual Variations: Sex and the Unmarried." pp. 152-179.
Payne, Dorothy. *Women Without Men: Creative Living for Singles, Divorcees, and Widows*. Philadelphia: Pilgrim Press, 1969.
Potts, Nancy. *Counseling with Single Adults*. Nashville: Broadman Press, 1978.
Reed, Bobbie. *Stepfamilies Living in Christian Harmony*. St. Louis: Concordia, 1980.
Sands, Audrey Lee. *Single and Satisfied*. Wheaton: Tyndale, 1971.
Scanzoni, John and Letha. *Men, Women and Change*. St. Louis: McGraw/Hill, 1976.
Scanzoni, Letha and Nancy Hardesty. *All We're Meant to Be*. Waco, Tex.: Word Books, 1974. See chapter twelve on "The Single Women" pp. 145-168.
Small, Dwight Hervey. *The Right to Remarry*. Old Tappan, N.J.: Revell, 1975.
Smedes, Lewis B. *Sex for Christians: The Limits and Liberties of Sexual Living*. Grand Rapids: Eerdmans, 1976. See part two, "Sex and Single People," pp. 107-150.
Smith, Harold Ivan. *A Part of Me Is Missing*. Irvine, Calif.: Harvest

House, 1979.

Sroka, Barbara. *One Is a Whole Number*. Wheaton: Victor Books, 1980.

Staples, Robert. *The World of Black Singles: Changing Patterns of Male/Female Relationships*. Westport, Conn.: Greenwood Press, 1981.

Start, Clarissa. *On Becoming a Widow*. St. Louis: Concordia, 1973.

Stein, Peter J. *Single*. Englewood Cliffs, N.J.: Prentice-Hall, 1976.

_____, ed. *Single Life: Unmarried Adults in Social Context*. New York: St. Martins Press, 1981.

The Catholic Theological Society of America. *Human Sexuality: New Directions in American Catholic Thought*. New York: Doubleday & Company, Inc., 1979. See section five, "Pastoral Guidelines: . . . Nonmarital Sexuality," pp. 174-244.

Towns, Jim, ed. *Solo Flight: 12 Personal Perspectives on the Single Life*. Wheaton: Tyndale, 1981.

Vetter, Bob and June. *Jesus Was a Single Adult*. Elgin, Ill.: D. C. Cook Co., 1978.

Wiebe, Katie F. *Alone: A Widow's Search for Joy*. Wheaton, Ill.: Tyndale, 1976.

Wilkie, Jane. *The Divorced Woman's Handbook: An Outline for Starting the First Year Alone*. New York: William Morrow, 1980.

Wood, Britton. *Single Adults Want to Be the Church Too*. Nashville: Broadman Press, 1978.

Periodicals

"Celebrate Singleness—Marriage May Be Second Best," *Christianity Today*, Vol. 20 (May 7, 1976), pp. 26-27.

Andrews, Sherry, "Why Is the Church Becoming Single Minded," *Charisma* (May 1981), pp. 32-37.

Beachy, Bertha, coordinator, "Singleness and Single Parenting" *MCC Peace Section on Women in Church and Society* (Nov.-Dec., 1981, issue).

Bixler, Ruth Ann, "Stereotypes," *The Mennonite*, Vol. 92 (May 24, 1977), p. 351.

Brumbaugh, Doris M., "I Am Not a Mother," *Messenger*, Vol. 119 (May 1970), p. 28.

Catoir, E. Wakin, "Unmatched Freedom of Unmarried Christians," *U.S. Catholic*, Vol. 45 (January 80), pp. 33-38.

Christman, Marge, "Building A Singles Ministry," *Vine Life*, Vol. 1 (May/June 1979), pp. 17-18.

Clarkson, Margaret, "Singleness: His Share for Me," *Christianity Today*, Vol. 23, (Feb. 16, 1979), pp. 14-15.

Clarkson, Margaret, "Life in Its Fullness," *Mennonite Brethren Herald*, Vol. 16 (Nov. 11, 1977), pp. 6-7.

Compton, Glenn L., "Christian Singles," *Evangelical Visitor*, Vol. 92 (June 25, 1979), p. 13.

Eck, Rodney, "Single, but Not Alone," *The Mennonite*, Vol. 93 (October 10, 1978), pp. 594-595.

Faith at Work magazine. October 1974 issue on singleness.

Forbes, Cheryl, "Let's Not Shackle the Single Life," *Christianity Today*, Vol. 22 (February 16, 1979), pp. 16-19.

Frost, Heidi, "'Tis a Gift to Be Single," *Evangelical Visitor*, Vol. 39 (July 10, 1976), p. 12.

Funk, Herta, "Images of Singleness," *The Mennonite*, Vol. 90 (October 7, 1975), pp. 557-558.

_____, "Single Is Whole," *With*, Vol. 9, (April 1976).

Gish, Dorothy J., "Single, Sane, and Satisfied," *Mennonite Medical Messenger*, (April-June 1979), Vol. 10-15, pp. 17, 26.

Ginder, Glenn, "Jesus: The Single Perspective," *Evangelical Visitor*, Vol. 90 (Feb. 10, 1977), pp. 10, 14.

Guentert, Kenneth, "25 Things Your Parish Can Do Before Starting a Singles Group," *U.S. Catholic*, Vol. 43 (April 1978), pp. 30-32.

Harms, Betty, "Finding Ourselves Complete," *The Mennonite*, Vol. 93 (November 14, 1978), pp. 658-659.

Jares, Sue Ellen, "Saturday Nights Can Be Tough, But to Author Lynn Shahan Living Alone Is the Best Revenge," *People*, Vol. 16, pp. 103-104.

Kehler, Larry, "One Face of Loneliness," *The Mennonite*, Vol. 91 (January 20, 1976), p. 48.

Klopfenstein, Janette, "Living Alone in a Couple's World," *Evangelical Visitor*, Vol. 89 (Feb. 25, 1976), pp. 12-13.

LeSourd, Linda, "The Single Woman and the Church," *The Mennonite Brethren Herald*, Vol. 16 (Nov. 11, 1977), pp. 2-4.

Maust, John "SALT I Gives New Visibility to Single Adult Ministries," *Christianity Today*, Vol. 24 (March 7, 1980), pp. 56, 58.

Meyer, Lauree Hercsh and Graydon Smith, "Sexuality: Its Social Reality and Theological Understanding in I Corinthians 7," Society of Biblical Literature, *Seminar Papers*, 1980.

Miller, Shari, "Singleness Is a Kingdom Option," *Christian Living*, Vol. 26 (September 1979), pp. 6-9.

Pierre, Janet Fix, "Enjoy Being Single—Now!" *Today's Christian Woman*, Vol. 1 (Fall 1979), pp. 33-34.

Schumm, Clare, "The Gift to Be Single," *Gospel Herald*, Vol. LXIX (March 23, 1976), pp. 238-239.

Schwartzentruber, Mary Mae, "Even If I Stay Single Forever," *Christian Living*, Vol. 27 (March 1980), pp. 25-27.

Shriner, Stephen L., "Singled Out," *Gospel Herald*, Vol. LXIX (March

23, 1976), p. 239.

Repohl, Roga, "The Spirituality of Singleness," *America*, Vol. 135 (Nov. 27, 1976), pp. 365-367.

Smith, Harold I., "Sex and Singleness the Second Time Around," *Christianity Today*, Vol. 23 (May 25, 1979), pp. 16-22.

Smoke, Jim, "Single, but Not Alone," *Evangelical Visitor*, Vol. 90 (July 25, 1977), pp. 12-13.

Stormer, Kathy, "Breakdown or Breakthrough," *The Mennonite*, Vol. 94 (September 11, 1979), pp. 532-533.

Strauss, Richard L., "The Family Church: Any Place for Singles?" *Christianity Today*, Vol. 21 (July 29, 1977), pp. 12-14.

"The Way 'Singles' Are Changing U.S.," *U.S. News and World Report*, Vol. 82 (Jan. 31, 1977), pp. 59-60.

Weaver, Mary Jo, "The Pain of Negative Definitions: Single Blessedness?" *Commonweal*, Vol. 106 (Oct. 26, 1979), pp. 588-591.

Wiebe, Katie Funk, "Pushed Out of the Ark," *The Mennonite*, Vol. 90 (Oct. .7, 1975), pp. 554-556.

Wiebe, Katie, "The Big 'X'," *Gospel Herald*, Vol. LXXII (May 15, 1979), p. 399.

Additional Resources

Solo (The Christian magazine for Single Adults) is a nondenominational magazine for singles which is published bimontly. It includes a wide range of articles and calendar events for singles. Order from Solo Ministries, 8740 E. 11th, Suite Q, Tulsa, OK 74112. Subscription $12.00 a year (subject to change).

The National Association of Christian Singles, (NACS) is a membership organization with divisions for singles, leaders, and chapters. NACS publishes a quarterly tabloid newspaper for singles, *Today's Single*, and a monthly newsletter for single or single adult leaders, *Single i*. *Today's Single*, which costs $4.00 a year, includes articles on singleness, and *Single i*, which costs $10.00 a year, lists the latest Christian literature pertaining to singleness and serves as a clearinghouse for singles concerns and activities. (Note, prices are subject to change.) Order from P.O. Box 11394, Kansas City, MO 64112.

The Writers

Herta Funk is director of adult education for the Commission on Education of the General Conference Mennonite Church, Newton, Kansas.

Dorothy Gish is a professor of education at Messiah College, Grantham, Pennsylvania.

Lois Janzen is a minister of the Haight-Ashbury Mennonite Fellowship in San Francisco, California.

Mel Lehman is director of the information office of Church World Service's Immigration and Refugee Program, New York City.

Martha Smith Good, of New Hamburg, Ontario, is a homemaker and minister of a church fellowship in Guelph, Ontario.

Bruce Yoder is pastor of the First Mennonite Church of Richmond, Virginia.

Imo Jeanne Yoder is a professor in the social work department of Eastern Mennonite College, Harrisonburg, Virginia, and plans to begin training in hospital chaplaincy.